Dedicated to making leadership as effective and satisfying as the quest for it —

Robert L. DeBruyn

TABLE OF CONTENTS

CAUSING OTHERS TO WANT YOUR LEADERSHIP

ROBERT L. DE BRUYN
AUTHOR OF THE MASTER TEACHER

R. L. DE BRUYN & ASSOCIATES
PUBLISHER
MANHATTAN, KANSAS

R. L. DE BRUYN & ASSOCIATES
Publisher
Leadership Lane
Manhattan, Kansas 66502

Library of Congress Catalog Card Number: 76-29223
ISBN 0-914607-06-5
First Printing 1976
Second Printing 1979
Third Printing 1983
Fourth Printing 1985
Printed in the United States of America

Part Two
YOU AND HUMAN MANAGEMENT

Part Three
YOU AND A LEADERSHIP PLAN

INTRODUCTION

There are two distinct sides to leadership and management. One side has to do with "things" and is called technical management. The other side of management has to do with leading people. The technical side of management includes such "things" as books, desks, chairs, buildings, land, budget preparation, purchasing, physical plant maintenance, and scheduling. As school administrators, we are usually well-versed and proficient on the "thing" side of management. We should be, for here we have been well-schooled by the colleges, universities, and professional organizations. In addition, we have kept pace on the "thing" side of management with our own programs and studies of learning and self-growth.

**OUR
BIGGEST
VOID**

The technical side of management is not my major concern in this book. I am concerned with the "people side" of management. Herein lies our biggest void as leaders in schools and school systems. It is also the area of management that produces most of our difficult, frustrating, and seemingly insolvable problems. The "people side" of management is of paramount importance to administrators, because, in the leadership plan, people are always more significant than "things." In truth, people are always both more constructive and destructive than all the various "things" which are included on the technical side of management.

ADDITIONAL ADMINISTRATIVE HANDICAPS

When this truth is coupled with the fact that administrators face countless tasks and problems inherent in leadership responsibility on the "people side" of management — ranging from students to the public — as well as the accountability for the accomplishment of all the work of the school, you have the makings of one of the most difficult and demanding positions in management today. Unlike most managers, a school administrator does not lead a particular group. He is not accountable only to owners or a board of directors like his corporate management counterpart. A school administrator must lead and is accountable to a host of people including students, teachers, secretaries, custodians, cooks, and the rest of the wide range of personnel that make up a school and district staff. He is also responsible and accountable to the central office, board of education, parents, public, and many, many other interest groups which are concerned with the work of the school.

In addition, the full power held by corporate management is not possessed by the principal or superintendent. Due process, teacher organizations, and outside groups limit the power of school administrators and the extension of that power. Even though unions are part of corporate management's power curtailment, educational management does not have the management-employee separation and protection enjoyed by corporate management. Principals and superintendents are much more vulnerable personally as a result of their position than are the management people in industry. That's why school administrators must be highly skilled on the human side of leadership.

TWO
KINDS
OF PROBLEMS

The technical side of management has presented us with many problems. But these are different kinds of problems than those related to leading people. Problems on the technical side of management are the same for all organizations, whether the organization is an industry, business, church, school, or family. For instance, resources for any organization will always be limited. Schools are not the exception. This is a problem in getting the work of the school accomplished that all can see and understand. The technical side of management reveals quickly our competency regarding decisions of sound allocation of resources which are in agreement with good management practices. But this is not, regardless of what one might think, the primary source of our frustrations, disappointments, failures, and criticisms as school leaders. Our real problems lie on the human side of leadership. That's why every school administrator must be as competent on the human side of management as he is on the technical side. If he is not, only half the job gets done. Worse, the half that gets done will offer few leadership rewards. The "people side" of management is where the satisfaction and rewards lie. It is also the real source of leadership respect. The reason is obvious. Success on the people side of management is what distinguishes a leader as exceptional.

ASSET
AND
LIABILITY

None would deny that the quality of any professional staff — from custodian to teacher — is our biggest administrative asset. However, people can be our greatest leadership obstacle. Things are always easier to manage because they cannot plot, scheme, blame, balk, second-guess, stall, procrastinate, destroy, or criticize. People do these things. But also, things cannot help, praise, create, work, or share. People can.

The purpose of this book is threefold. First, it will familiarize administrators with the wants, needs, and motivations of hu-

Causing
Others
to Want
Your
Leadership

man beings. This foundation is necessary for all in leadership positions. Second, it will introduce school administrators to the Laws, Principles, and Theories of Human Management as they relate to being school administrators and to leading people. Third, this book will provide administrators with the practical and workable methods, techniques, and skills needed to lead people in agreement with good management practices. Hopefully, this book will give administrators the repertoire of skills needed to become as proficient on the people side of management as they are on the technical side. This book goes beyond defining the problem. It gives some answers which can be applied — immediately.

PART ONE

YOU AND PEOPLE

WHAT LEADERSHIP IS

People usually get to be leaders because they were good "doers." They were good teachers, or counselors, or coaches. They were elevated through the ranks of the school organization because someone noted their potential. Most often, they demonstrated the ability to do a good job as educators, and someone promoted their potential. Yet, a good "doer" does not necessarily mean someone will be a good leader. Management is a whole new "ball game." That's why there are two important questions that need answering by everyone in or aspiring to hold an administrative position. The first question I will answer for you. The other, you will have to answer for yourself. The questions are:

1. What is leadership?
2. Are you a leader?

As certainly as some men and women have aspired to be leaders, others have been inspired by leadership. At some point in our lives, many of us have had someone who influenced and changed our lives and careers in either a positive, constructive way — or a negative, destructive way. Without doubt, those who inspire are those with a special ability to relate to and motivate others. More often than not, consciously or subconsciously, they apply the Laws and Principles of both leadership and management to the motivation of human beings in a very human way. They realize, above all else, that leadership is a function rather than a position. This seems to be their common thread. This attitude toward being in a leadership position is a must. The principalship is not a position; it is a function. The superintendency is not a position; it is a function. Leadership is a function.

There are many long and complex definitions of the word **leadership.** Men and women have argued endlessly over minor points in the definition of the word and made long lists of what a leader is and is not and what a leader should or should not be. Unfortunately, too many people in leadership positions are never able to move past their definition to lead people and get the work of the school accomplished.

SIMPLE . . .
YET
ALL-INCLUSIVE

I choose to define leadership simply as: "causing others to want what you are doing to accomplish the work of the school." Close examination should prove that this definition is all-inclusive. It is assumed, of course, that the leader is striving to meet the objectives of the institution. It is also assumed within this definition that a leader is doing nothing by word or deed which is contrary to the reasons for the creation or existence of the institution.

For example, a school must be student-centered. Meeting the needs of students is the reason for the creation and existence of schools. Schools employ teachers, nurses, counselors, administrators, cooks, custodians and many others. Yet, a leader should not and cannot expect to "cause teachers to want what you are doing" if leadership priorities and efforts are "in the best interest of administrators," but not the best interest of students. Leadership efforts must be in agreement with the reason for the existence of the institution, or leadership efforts will not be accepted. They may not even be tolerated.

WANT
IS
THE KEY

The key word in this definition of leadership is **want.** This word in the body of the definition makes both leading and being led a rewarding experience. The word **want** automatically excludes such leadership practices as being dictatorial, self-centered, belligerent, or protecting the status quo. Why? Because people do not and will not ever come to a point of wanting what you are doing as a leader when these leadership characteristics are present.

The word **want** in this definition also changes the meaning of another word in the definition. Without the word **want,** one could easily be misled or misinterpret the word **causing.** In the day-to-day application of leadership, many administrators practice this definition without the words **causing** and **want** — and it gets them into trouble.

The word causing can imply pressure, force, coercion, and even fear. However, the word **want** in this definition eliminates all of these possibilities in leadership pratices. **Want** is an important word — it's a word that one aspiring to lead other human beings cannot and should not ever forget. Without this one word, caring might not be included in either leadership attitude or practice.

AN
ADVANTAGE
FROM BOTH SIDES

A close look will reveal that this definition of leadership is one that you — as an administrator — need very much to live by in more ways than one. Equally important, it is one that the vast majority of those you lead will need to live by too. It makes both leading and being led a satisfying, rewarding, productive, and beneficial experience both personally and professionally.

15

**EQUAL
COMPETENCY
ON THE HUMAN SIDE ...**

The way you "cause others to want what you are doing" is through a thorough understanding and deep, personal commitment to the Laws and Principles of Human Management. Unfortunately, not very many school administrators have been extensively exposed to the Laws and Principles of Management. Some may not even know what they are. There may even be some in education leadership positions who scoff at the Laws and Principles. Mostly, though, I hope school leaders fully realize that these Laws and Principles apply whenever one human being leads another. In addition, in the desire to find success for self as well as success for the institution, one of the reasons these Laws and Principles should be totally accepted and applied is that they make leading as well as being led a rewarding and fulfilling experience. This is important. If one cannot find happiness, fulfillment, and a sense of recognition from others for his or her leaderhip efforts, then leading is not worth the price one must pay personally and professionally for it.

It's a fact: leading can be a totally and overwhelmingly miserable experience. Being a school administrator can be the most lonely and thankless professional job in our country. As you know well, there are far too many school leaders "wishing they were out of the business" or "wanting to return to the classroom or another position with less pressure, fewer problems, and more appreciation and peace of mind." In large measure, these administrators' feelings and attitudes are the result of a void of skills on the human side of leadership. Much of this administrative despair is the product of being unprepared on the human side of management. Many school administrators were trained thoroughly on the technical side of administration, then given the keys to a building and forced to learn the human side of leadership alone.

**A
RESULT
OF OUR DEFICIENCIES**

In too many instances, negative staff members, outsiders,

and pressure groups have taken leadership away from us. Make no mistake, this has happened because we have allowed it to happen. We have allowed it because we didn't know how to stop it. One of the reasons for this dilemma is that we have not had the advantage of our corporate management colleagues. Business has extensive training programs for potential management candidates. There are continual workshops, seminars, and meetings to help their executives cope with problems on the human side of management. Not us. We have had to learn the vast majority of our skills on the human side of management through self-growth or trial and error. It has been a very difficult way to learn, and we have paid a heavy price for each of our mistakes. We may still be paying for ones we made years ago. Thankfully, it is never too late to begin anew. With a solid foundation, old mistakes are forgotten if new leadership ways contain good management and human relations practices.

TWO
COMMON
APPROACHES TO LEADERSHIP

Many people in management positions believe that there are basically only two ways to motivate human beings to want leadership direction and accept those in administrative positions. One, assuming you have the ability to lead, is to make it very pleasant for people to do the things you want them to do or move in the direction you want them to go, individually or collectively. Or, you can make it unpleasant for people not to do the things you want them to do or move in the direction you want them to go, individually or collectively.

My definition of leadership excludes the second choice of leadership direction. I believe if a teacher or staff member's behavior, attitude, or practices force an administrator to be unpleasant continually in order to motivate, termination must be considered. However, management must first do everything within their power to change a staff member's behavior, attitude, and practices before termination can be effected. This is leadership. If our efforts are not successful and we do not terminate, then care must be taken not to change our leadership personality or management practices in leading people.

We simply can't reveal one management philosophy when dealing with some people and another when dealing with others. It won't work. It is also dangerous because a leader can begin doing, saying, and acting in a manner which is contrary to good leadership practices.

ADMINISTRATIVE RELATIONSHIPS WITH ONE ... AFFECT RELATIONSHIPS WITH ALL

One must never forget that administrative action or nonaction taken with one employee affects the relationships with all employees. In the case of nonaction by management with the poor teacher, it weakens positive leadership efforts with all staff members.

Unfortunately, there are many leaders who have had so many bad experiences in their efforts to "make it pleasant for people to do what you want them to do" that they have come to believe the "you can't be nice to people." They believe a leader must carry a big stick and use or threaten to use it often to motivate people. When this is the adopted leadership attitude, leadership personality becomes negative. One begins leading toward the negative and away from the positive.

Fortunately, successful leaders believe this kind of leadership is not good for them, the institution, or those being led. Not only does it make being led a terrible experience, it makes leading more miserable. Those leaders who choose to abuse the power delegated to them and adopt a leadership philosophy and direction based on domination, fear, and mistreatment of those being led seldom find any degree of happiness and satisfaction in their life work. More important, they seldom survive in their positions of leadership over the long-term. In the years ahead they will find survival almost impossible. The only way they will manage to stay in administrative positions is to move continually from job to job and district to district.

A FAILURE-PRODUCING MISCONCEPTION

I've heard some school leaders in recent years express the

belief that a school administrator shouldn't plan to spend more than five years in any position in any system. School administration, they say, will require moving from location to location and position to position periodically throughout a career. The days of long tenure in one position, they say, are over. If you're one of these administrators, let me say this. The whole world isn't wrong. You are. This kind of thinking is ridiculous. No institution can progress with this type of leadership attitude or turnover. Schools are not the exception. What administrators need most is to develop and employ the leadership and management skills used to promote, facilitate, and maintain the motivation and cooperation of those being led. What we need to do is to learn how to "cause others to want what we are doing" by operating in a manner which allows this to become a reality. Certainly, this is easier said than done. But it can be accomplished with a firm knowledge, understanding, and employment of the Laws and Principles of Management as they relate to leading people.

COMMUNICATION IS A LEADERSHIP ABSOLUTE

The key to causing others to want what you are doing is communication. If you can't communicate with your people, you can't lead, much less cause others to want what you are doing. That's a pure, absolute, and unchangeable fact.

Yet, communication remains a constant administrative problem. Administrative communication helps to effect staff acceptance and understanding — and at every level of leadership responsibility, understanding seems to be a problem. This is revealed by everyone on all levels throughout the school and system. Everyone says the other doesn't understand.

Students say teachers and parents don't understand. Teachers say administrators don't understand. Administrators say teachers don't understand, and we all say the public doesn't understand. Worse, at each level of awareness, the problem is often met with a form of rationalization that the fault lies not with us — but with the one who does not understand.

A
MANAGEMENT
RESPONSIBILITY

In reality, it is the responsibility of leadership to "cause others to want what they are doing" to accomplish the work of the schools. This can only be achieved when leadership accepts the responsibility for this so-called "understanding problem," and then, through skilled communication and application of the Laws and Principles of Management, brings about understanding on every level inside and outside the institution. Understanding will never result without administrative and communicative action on a continuous basis.

That's not to say that communication will eliminate all misunderstandings. It will not. Breakdowns will occur along the way. This is not the issue. The issue is that when administrators do not accept the responsibility for communication, then a lack of understanding will become a permanent condition rather than a temporary situation. Some leaders may be disappointed when their efforts don't bring total and instant understanding. Some get angry about it. Some stop communicating. Yet, understanding is never total. However, without leadership communication, misunderstanding will be more common than understanding. Worse, it will become permanent. Make no mistake, both communication and being understood are the responsibility of management.

Certainly, problems in communication and understanding will always arise. But the constant reality of problems is never an allowable management excuse to shirk or rationalize away an administrative responsibility. The continuous emergence of the problems which result from both understanding and communication only serve to stress the fact that the need for management skill and expertise on the human side of management is an absolute. Without such a foundation, we must rely on trial-and-error techniques.

Trial-and-error management techniques always result in further misunderstanding. They cause institutions to regress, for it is always a matter of taking one step forward with every success and two steps backward with every failure. Trial-and-error techniques usually result in poor human relationships inside and outside the institution. On the other hand, the Laws and Principles of Management always give an administrator direction, as well as specific methods and techniques to employ in various situations with people. They provide a foundation of tried and tested expertise. The Laws and Principles of Management make every problem an opportunity for administrative success rather than another probability for administrative embarrassment and failure. They remove much of the trial and error from administrative decisions and courses of action. Equally important, the Laws and Principles give the foundation out of which those being led can follow. Management word and deed have meaning and reveal good judgment. Without doubt, the Laws and Principles of Management serve as the foundation for every beginning — in administrative attitude and perception as well as action.

A
BASE
OF ADMINISTRATIVE OBJECTIVITY

The Laws and Principles of Management also do much for one's self-confidence. They are objective, not subjective. And that's what every administrator needs in problem situations — objectivity. In truth, a good administrator always seems to turn a problem situation into one which is beneficial to all — students, school, and the parties involved. The administrator "looks good" because problem situations are handled in agreement with sound educational practices. There are good reasons this is so. It's not always personality. One can't always rely on charisma. Sound management principles must accompany an administrator's individual personality if success is to be achieved and sustained.

Once a leader accepts the responsibility for the understanding of all within his or her orbit, the entire administrative outlook as well as its perception and procedure are easily adjusted or changed. A good leader never says others are responsible for "not understanding." And his techniques to bring about "causing others to want what he is doing" include both the employment of sound management Laws and Principles as well as teaching those he leads by careful and planned explanations and communications. These administrative communications always utilize the Primary and Secondary human motivations and needs.

I will discuss the Primary and Secondary wants, needs, and motivations later. However, the first thing that must be considered is your personal and professional attitude toward leading as an administrator. Your leadership attitude begins by affirming and accepting the definition that leadership is ... "causing others to want what you are doing."

It is not "making" someone do anything. Neither does it involve "forcing" or "pressuring" someone to accept your leadership or threatening him in some way if he doesn't. Fear has no place in education. Administration is not the exception. This definition of leadership has no hidden meanings or interpretations. There's no club in this definition. But there is a great deal of empathy, persuasion, and teaching — without dictating.

We all want to be good administrators. We all want to do a good job. We want good schools and good school systems. We want to be inspiring, successful, and respected leaders. We want others to recognize our skills and appreciate our effectiveness. It can't be done with a club. It can be done only through understanding people and knowing how to motivate and communicate to them the needs of students while finding professional fulfillment in the process. It can only be achieved with sound administrative decisions which are in accordance with sound management practices.

ARE
YOU
A LEADER?

The second question which you must answer for yourself is: Are you a leader? When answering this question, there are some considerations you must recognize and deal with objectively.

Remember, the probability that you became an administrator because you were a good "doer." You might have been a great classroom teacher. Remember that the chances are great that this is the reason you are in the position you hold now — because that is how we choose our leaders. But just because you were a good teacher does not necessarily mean you are a good administrator. In fact, everything you did to find success as a teacher can work against your being a good leader.

Management is a new level of responsibility. It requires

changed abilities and actions — in attitude and thinking as well as work. Unless the "doer position" is dropped and the management position is assumed, a leader can operate in wrong ways and in wrong directions. Having been a good doer can result in your becoming what I call a "mechanical" manager once an administrative position is attained. For example, many leaders work very hard in their jobs. Yet, in truth, they are working hard doing their job in the same ways they did as a doer — and not doing the job they need to do as an administrator. They were such good "doers" that they can't allow themselves to be anything else. They like getting involved and "digging in" and actually doing a job. They can't let go. They can't delegate. They can't teach to do — they can only do. For instance, a teacher calls us to her classroom because she needs help, and we return to the classroom time and time again to restore order. As a result, we think we are leading. In fact, we like returning to do the kinds of things we did so well as a "doer." It makes us happy and fulfilled and gives us a feeling that we are, indeed, good leaders.

We are happy and pleased that our people need us. So time and time again we return to the task of a doer. We chair every meeting. We explain every proposal or idea at faculty meetings. We monitor restrooms and cafeterias rather than delegate. Then we mistakenly think people will be happy and pleased to see us "doing our job." In truth, our schools often have the highest paid custodian, cafeteria attendant, restroom watcher, and hall monitor in town — the administrator.

We are amazed that our efforts are not appreciated and recognized. Unfortunately, they never will be. Worse, we will be criticized. This is mechanical management. We are "doing" rather than delegating or helping others out of their problems and teaching them to be masters of their profession.

OUR
TASK
IS LEADING

As mechanical managers, we not only don't do our jobs, we don't allow others to become competent in their jobs. When we restore order in a classroom continually, does the teacher learn?

The answer is, no. In fact, our teachers may keep having the same problems. Our "doing" may weaken their position with students. Teachers may become dependent rather than self-sufficient because of our actions. We have not helped those we lead gain skills or confidence when we operate as mechanical managers.

Our task in leading is not to be a "doer" — but to help others become doers. Unfortunately, in many ways we may derive satisfaction from "doing" these kinds of experiences as administrators. It makes us feel we are worth more than we are getting paid. It makes us feel that the school needs us and couldn't operate without us. And, it makes us feel that we are doing a great job by what we are doing. Why? Quite frankly, because we do these things so well. We are the "best doer" in our school, but we are not a leader. Then, when we are criticized for not being a good administrator, we can't understand why. We need to understand that the reason our performance does not bring respect is that we are still doing those tasks that gave us the opportunity to be a leader — but we aren't doing those things leaders are supposed to do. In fact, we may even think more like a doer than a leader. In many, many ways the help given by a mechanical manager is degrading to those being led. More often than not, rather than appreciate administrative help, they are likly to form the opinion that you, as their leader, do not have the ability to lead. They may think you also believe that "nobody can do things right, except you." They are also prone to believe that you do not respect or appreciate them.

You are now management. Now you must concentrate on the tasks of an administrator — not on the tasks of a doer. You must teach those you lead to handle the situations which they must face. We, as school administrators, are a teacher of doers. But we are not doers. If we are, then we are merely mechanical managers.

A
NEW
LEVEL OF COMPETENCY

Our level of success as leaders will be determined by how

well we motivate and assist others in the attainment of professional excellence. It will also be determined by how well we
teach those we lead to solve problems and how well we resolve
problems ourselves. That's why to achieve leadership success,
one must develop a logical and effective method of resolving
each difficulty faced. This can only be achieved by adjusting
our behavior or position to get others to adjust their behavior or
position. This is how management changes negatives to positives. This is called Situation Management.

This is our goal as administrators, whenever possible. We
want to change problem situations into positives. Second, we
want to learn how to prevent these problem situations from
occurring again. This can never be achieved by mechanical
management.

WHAT
ARE
SITUATIONS?

Situations are occurrences which cause us to be faced with
action decisions to return our life and the life of those we lead
to the status which existed prior to the occurrence. If possible,
we want to improve our position and help others improve
theirs. Remember, situations are opportunities for either administrative failure or success.

Because we are human beings, we encounter at least three
personal and professional reactions and behaviors in every
problem-solving situation.

First, we usually have a tendency to react defensively. This is
a common human response. It is not abnormal. However, it is
not professional. When we automatically think that problems
reflect upon us personally, our efforts as administrators can
easily be devoted entirely to trying to absolve ourselves of both
the problem and everything related to it. Unfortunately, when
this administrative behavior results, we abandon and withdraw
ourselves from our leadership position. We can neither avoid a
problem situation nor react to it personally or defensively. We
must react professionally. If a doctor told me to lose twenty
pounds and I did not, he would not react as if I had offended
him. He would react professionally. Therefore, he is still in a

position to help me with **my** problem.

As professional administrators, when we react personally and defensively to problems, we are likely to try to absolve ourselves of all responsibility during the problem situation. Then it is impossible to try to return to a position of leadership after the conflict passes. We won't act as if nothing has happened if we remember that leadership acceptance and competency is not really measured before or after a problem situation. It is measured during it. That's when opinions are formed — they are simply utilized as reference points at other times by those being led. They remember "what happened" the last time and anticipate what might happen the next time by how an administrator reacted "during" the crisis.

Second, most people have a tendency not to face the reality that most adverse situations are, at least partially, created by them. Administrators are not the exception. This tendency is caused when we fail to accept the management law called the Law of Total Responsibility, which we will talk about later. However, if a leader accepts the definition of leadership which includes "causing others to want," then he can willingly accept the damage this common human tendency can cause both to him and those he leads. When it is not accepted, problems don't get solved; they just get blamed on someone.

Finally, many leaders fail to know, understand, and appreciate the behavior and motivations of themselves and those they lead. That's why a brief study of the wants, needs, and motivations of human beings must be included in this book. Before the rationale for the Laws and Principles of Human Management can be fully grasped, and then applied, we must come to a greater appreciation of not only what motivates our staff to act as they do, but also what motivates us, as leaders, to act and think as we do.

CHAPTER

2

UNDERSTANDING HUMAN BEHAVIOR

Just as we are all different and unique as human beings, we are all amazingly alike. As educators, we should know this better than most. We were once classroom teachers. We understand individual differences. We've been schooled about the "whole" child. We've studied individualized instruction. We have been and are committed to meeting the needs of students. Stepping into an administrative position only broadens our scope. In many ways, we need to apply what we learned in the classroom as teachers working with students to our task of administration in working with the staff. There is a parallel. As teachers, and now as administrators, we must understand the wants, needs, and motivations of people.

Certain wants and needs motivate and dictate human behavior. Most important to a leader, these wants and needs are absolutes. That makes them predictable. To write an entire book on the Laws and Principles of Management as related to the task of being a school administrator without devoting time to this vital aspect of human behavior would be like going fishing without a hook. We would, in truth, find all the right answers but hear the wrong questions. When studying the

Understanding
Human
Behavior

Laws and Principles of Management, hopefully you will readily agree that inherent in their content are all the human wants, needs, and motivators. That's why the Laws and Principles work.

PHYSIOLOGICAL
AND
PSYCHOLOGICAL

Psychology has traditionally classified human behavior into two major categories, Primary and Secondary Motives. A clear understanding of the meaning and implications of these motives is vital for any administrator who truly wants to practice Human Management, because the motives are part of us all; only their arrangement in terms of individual intensities and priorities varies. Before looking at them individually, let's look at them collectively to aid understanding.

PRIMARY MOTIVES
(Physiological and Unlearned)

1. Hunger
2. Thirst
3. Sex
4. Air
5. Rest
6. Escape pain
7. Eliminate Waste

SECONDARY OR DERIVED MOTIVES
(Psychological or Learned)

1. Gregariousness
2. Aggression
3. Affiliations
4. Inquisitiveness
5. Achievement
6. Power
7. Status
8. Autonomy

I suspect that you can think of the name of a teacher, secretary, counselor, cook, custodian, nurse, or administrator and see which needs are more intensely revealed in some than others. Too, you might realize that if you tried to fulfill these needs, you might have been more successful in an administrative effort involving them. By meeting these needs for someone, you could have changed a negative attitude or situation into a positive one. You are probably right in your assumption. That's how vital these motives are to leadership efforts. They are your first consideration in leading people. Ignoring these wants and needs as a leader will result in moving to step two in the leadership effort before you have covered step one.

An awareness of these motives is paramount to all human relationships. They apply to every employee — those we reach as well as those we do not. That's important because even if we are successful with the majority of our staff, it is our failure with a few that can cause us so much frustration, disappointment, and grief. Yet, overlooking the Primary and Secondary Motives is often the reason behind many of our leadership failures. More often than not, our failures have nothing to do with us. They have to do with the other person. Our failure comes in not recognizing a motive and adjusting our behavior, technique, and procedure as a result of that revealed or identified motive. Rather, we plow ahead, aware of our own needs and oblivious to the wants, needs, and motives of others. The result is failure.

Failure as a leader can bring us many negative emotions. When we are not accepted as a leader, we might begin to think that we alone are the entire problem. Often we are; yet as I said, just as often we are not. That's why we must make an individual interpretation of the Primary and Secondary Motives a part of every staff relationship and every leadership action.

29

Remember, the Primary Motives are physiological and un-learned. They are inherent in our being. In the hierarchy of human needs, these needs **must** be fulfilled before anything else can receive a teacher's attention. Without reservation, they must be fulfilled before the Secondary Motives can even be considered by an individual. This is of utmost importance because it is within the Secondary needs that most motives for professional excellence and the motivation to follow leadership exist.

Hopefully, one can see that if a teacher comes to school fearful, tired, or with the countless problems that can exist at home — school and the demands of school are of minor or even insignificant importance. In fact, they can foster strong and forceful resentments. The void of the fulfillment of a Primary Motive can cause hate for administrators, the work of the school, the happiness of more fortunate colleagues, and even resentment and bitterness toward happy and successful children. An unfulfilled Primary Motive can breed negative and antiprofessional attitudes. Then, having an administrator who seems oblivious to this personal void and is urging one to "meet the needs of students" or "accomplish the work of the school" can produce a wide variety of feelings — and none of them are good. It's not difficult to see why. That teacher who is having a marital problem at home is going to bring that discomfort to school. And we, as administrators, will be faced with the challenge to judiciously handle the situation. Sometimes we forget the strength of these Primary wants in relating to and motivating those we lead. We might even believe the Primary Motives aren't our problem. They are.

Look closely; those one or two staff members who are giving you the most trouble may be struggling in an attempt to gain fulfillment of a Primary need. You may be able to help — sometimes simply by demonstrating an awareness of their situation or by giving gentle consideration — and turn the situation around. Certainly teachers are reminded to be aware of the Primary Motives in their classroom relationship with students. Likewise, administrators need to be aware of them in relation to teachers too. More importantly, administrators need to act toward and out of the Primary Motives in effecting leadership and establishing their relationship with staff members.

PSYCHOLOGICAL
AND
LEARNED

There is simply no way an administrator can lead without an awareness and thorough knowledge of the Secondary Motives. They are the foundation of human motivation. Called derived motives, they are psychological and learned. Remember this fact: they are learned. Although the degree of intensity and priority may vary from human to human, they too are within us all.

THE
SECONDARY OR
DERIVED MOTIVES

It is within the Secondary Motives that people reach their goals and raise their self-concept. People with a high intensity of Secondary needs are highly motivated. They are likely to be successful as well. Those with a low intensity are likely to be under-achievers and have a low self-concept. Without a doubt, teachers with a low-concept are unlikely to excel or be of much value to anyone — students and the work of the school included. They may passively follow leadership, but they will not make a significant contribution to educational excellence or efficiency in getting the work of the school accomplished. Unfortunately, they are often the source of administrative failure as well as their own. Because teachers with a low-intensity of Secondary needs can be led very easily, leaders often surround themselves with them. That's a mistake, but it is also a reality. When we promote those with weak motivation and low self-concept because they continually tell us how good we are or because they never challenge our leadership, we surround ourselves with weakness. Staff weakness is administrative weakness. No leader can be any better than the potential of those being led. When we promote weakness in any way, we also take on the responsibility for any failures which result. That's a fact.

Teachers with a low self-concept are nurtured with weak leadership. They are a primary source of problems for schools and administrators — even if we have never thought about it in this way. People with a strong self-concept make the best colleagues and classroom teachers.

The Secondary Motives are extremely strong forces in the lives of the highly motivated. To be a dynamic and positive leader, one must appeal not only to those needs in the highly motivated, but also set a course of action which will stimulate those needs in the less motivated. When we do, we achieve the maximum utilization of personnel and maximum effort per task. Remember there are eight Secondary Motives. They are:

1. Gregariousness. This is the need people have to associate with a group. Because a faculty must operate so often as a team, an administrator must meet and nurture this need to fulfillment. This motive is easily evidenced by teachers who have strong desires for inclusion in the "inner circle" with those who administer an institution. This is also the motive that causes teachers to be upset if left off a committee, not asked to attend a meeting, or not told about the decision to do something. This is one reason "read-and-route" types of communication offend and "hurt" many people.

2. Aggression. People have a need to assert themselves. A leader must allow people to fulfill this need, or leadership will often be fought rather than accepted. Inclusion in certain decisions, involvement in planning activities, and responsibility for choosing specific courses of action are good administrative outlets which can be employed to meet this need. Teachers have one prerogative in their favor which leaders should frequently act upon to fulfill the need for aggression: academic freedom. The fact that teachers do have freedom to operate in many ways as a separate entity within the whole of the school should be stressed by leaders. Herein lies an advantage in teaching not offered by many of the professions. It meets a high individual need that leaders should point out in a positive way as often as possible.

3. Affiliations. Developing, maintaining, and strengthen-
ing associations with other individuals is a strong human
need. This need is accented on the professional level.
Teachers need to be close to each other, but they often
also have an intense desire to be "close" to the boss.
Never forget this truth. Interschool and intersystem activities are always a good administrative practice. Activities ranging from socials to curriculum planning should
be a part of the leadership plan, or a big void in meeting
this need may result. Union leaders are masters at developing and meeting this Secondary need. Simple observation will reveal that union management has perfected
the "all for one, one for all" procedure in effecting
leadership on a real-life level.

4. Inquisitiveness. People need to know what is going on.
It's a strong need. The more they are involved in an
activity or institution, the more evident this need appears. This need has been expressed more forcefully in
recent years because people want to fulfill the need to
control their own lives. The leader who "fights" the
fulfillment of this need may encounter unlimited difficulty. Sometimes when we think someone is being
"nosy," we "turn him off." That's a leadership mistake.
People are motivated by a need to know. It is this
motivation which brings learning. People also have a
drive to know how you feel about them — as people —
as well as professional teachers. This is one reason we
need a continuous communication with those we lead.
Teachers need weekly bulletins, intercom announcements, administrative briefings, and regular department
meetings as planned outlets to meet this need of inquisitiveness. However, our communication must also tell
those we lead that we are concerned for them personally
and professionally in addition to revealing administrative plans. Equally important, administrative communication should reveal the "whys" behind what we are
doing and the decisions we have made. This need is
easily met by management. There is simply no excuse
for not filling it. Those leaders who are secretive and
withhold basic information act contrary to a human
motive which will prove detrimental to both the leader
and the leadership practice. You can count on it.

5. Achievement. All people need to succeed and be recognized for their success. As leaders, we must recognize that success without recognition weakens the motivation. No accomplishment should go unnoticed. As leaders, our recognition of the achievement of our staff is one of the most important things that we do. Certainly, parents and students don't give teachers enough appreciation and recognition for their achievements in the classroom. We must never forget that failure offers no motivation at all. People are not motivated by their failures. They are motivated by their successes. That's why a leader must never forget that people don't like to do what they do poorly. They like to do what they do well. Sometimes, people won't even "try" what they can't do well. We need to remember this Secondary need the next time we are trying to unite a staff toward accepting a new procedure or increasing their productivity.

6. Power. This need can be a positive or a negative. Yet, it is a strong need. What a leader should recognize is that people need to know that they count. This is a form of power. Making those being led feel significant is an absolute in meeting this human need. Equally important, a leader cannot ever try to eliminate power from the base of people's needs. We do this every time we give responsibility for a task without granting the degree of authority required to achieve success with the task. Never forget, titles are important in filling the power need, but so is the authority and responsibility which goes with the title. When you give both while assigning tasks, you get things done and provide an individual with both the individual motivation and satisfaction needed in the process.

7. Status. Everybody wants to be a somebody. Any dehumanizing effort or action by leadership is a mistake. Nothing should ever be done that detracts from the identity of the individual. Don't ever think individual identities can't be met in a group work. They can. In fact, it's the different kinds of individual skills and strengths within a group that make all group endeavors successful. The challenge of leadership is to combine the needs of the individual with the needs of the institution.

Some might say this is "picking the right people for the right job." This is only partially true. The good leader can make the majority good for the task that needs to be accomplished. This can only be achieved by fulfilling the needs of people in the process of meeting the needs of tasks.

8. Autonomy. We all want to be our own boss, don't we? We want our own way. We'll talk about this need in depth later. It's one of our strongest motivators. It can be among a leader's greatest assets in achieving the work of the school.

We should remember that the Secondary Motives, as the Primary Motives, apply not only to our staff and associates, but also apply most pointedly to us as well. The needs that motivate other people to do what they do are the same needs that motivate us. The full realization of this truth is a major ingredient for Human Management.

A
CONTINUOUS
STUDY

The Primary and Secondary wants and needs provide a school administrator with invaluable leadership insights. They are the clues to all human behavior. They tell us why people think and act the way they do. An administrator could spend an entire lifetime studying each of these Primary and Secondary needs and applying them to all within the school orbit — from student, to teacher, to parent, to himself. I suggest you do. The Primary and Secondary needs would make an excellent topic for a seminar or workshop.

These learned and unlearned motives must never be ignored or overlooked by any administrator in either individual or group leadership endeavors. They are the key that unlocks the door to individual and group motivation actions and reactions. Every administrator should study and learn every facet and interpretation of these motives as they relate to his or her leadership group. Without giving the Primary and Secondary Motives attention, one may find that orders, commands, and directives are an absolute necessity in achieving every leadership desire. We may find "causing others to want" an impossibility. If, by chance, we treat these Primary and Secondary Motives as unimportant, we may find mass dissent and even insubordination at our door. We should also remember that staff dissent and insubordination need not be out in the open to be in existence. Fear may keep it hidden. Yet, at the first sign of opportunity or administrative weakness, we may find an explosion we cannot control.

A lack of management awareness of the Primary and Secondary Motives is likely to lead to a great management misconception: we tend to believe that all whom we lead are alike. We tend to stereotype all teachers, cooks, custodians, counselors, and others into neat little packages. We are also prone to believe that all teachers are equal. They are not. People are not equal in their experience, ability, or motivation. They are all different. The priorities of their wants and needs vary. What is important to one is not to another. All of our teachers are products of their environment and their experiences — past, present, and anticipated. That's why these motives are the first place an administrator must look when leadership efforts are being approved and accepted — or ignored and rejected. Remember, rejection of leadership may be professional. However, more often than not it is personal — absolutely and totally personal. That's why so many rejections of leadership seem irrational and without solution. They are if you are looking in the wrong places for the right answers. That's what makes leading difficult and frustrating. That's what also makes it interesting, fascinating, challenging, and tremendously rewarding.

It is your ability to "cause others to want" that has allowed you the opportunity to lead. Your actions must be rational and objective. Your actions must also rest on a base of administrative knowledge and skill. If you don't make the Primary and Secondary Motives a part of your leadership skills — you can't be using good judgment in many situations.

A study of human behavior could stop here. The Primary and Secondary Motives are all-inclusive. However, I believe there is a real necessity to delve more deeply and comprehensively into the implications of the Secondary Motives, specifically as they relate to school administration; for the majority of problem situations that you will experience with people are rooted in these Motives. A fuller understanding of the Secondary Motives is a major key to effective leadership through Human Management.

3

THE
PRIORITIES
OF PEOPLE

In this chapter, we will look more closely into the implications of the Secondary Motives by describing the Nine Priorities that cause people to be the way they are. A clear understanding of these Priorities will benefit your leadership activity in three significant ways:

1. They will help you to understand what people's actions **really** mean, rather than what they **appear** to mean.
2. They will help you to react **objectively** in a problem situation, rather than **subjectively.**
3. They will help you view a problem situation **professionally**, rather than **personally.**

Let's consider these Nine Priorities relative to our staff as well as ourselves:

1. Esteem and Love. All of us have a strong need to feel good about who we are, what we are, and where we are. But as administrators, it should be apparent who among our teachers and staff members **crave** esteem, status, and prestige. For example, those who fight and engage in

political battles to be department heads or chairmen of committees, even when they are not wanted, crave status. Likewise, when some teachers feel they are not being respected by students, they may act in ways that are completely contrary to everything they have learned as professionals; such conduct is also a clear manifestation of need for esteem. People who seek personal status often desire that others view them as "achievers." An "achiever" may be the individual who wants to be a recognized authority, or one who always strives to accomplish something significant and important, or one who thrives on doing a difficult job well. In any event, we should realize that whenever we can make it possible for such individuals to actually fulfill their need, our leadership will become welcomed and supported.

Many administrators have not considered the fact that at the very heart of a desire for esteem often lies a longing for love and a feeling of belonging. This fundamental need frequently surfaces only as the desire for status or prestige. The staff members who constantly stop to see us may not only be looking for esteem and recognition, they may also need a gesture of warmth and understanding from us. They may be seeking our support. This is the reason many staff members are offended if they can't see us whenever they wish or if they did not receive a copy of a bulletin or memo sent from the office. Our staff members want to form strong affiliations with each other and with us. Creating an environment which fulfills the need for esteem and love will make strong affiliations possible.

2. Predictability. The need for predictability refers to the desire to ally oneself with the familiar and, therefore, the secure. This is what causes teachers to like routine, insist upon planned schedules, and urge administrators to establish standard operating procedures for handling discipline problems and routine tasks. It's also the reason behind much of the rationale of the teacher who totally rejects anything new, complains about assemblies, criticizes unannounced intercom interruptions, and objects harshly to music, art, and other activities which cause students to be late for class or leave the room early. Although these kinds of interruptions are inherent in

schools, they will usually bring criticism of the activity and the administrator. Accepting the need teachers and other staff members have for predictability will insure that you communicate all changes in daily routine carefully and thoroughly to all the staff. It will also help you realize that advance notice and planning are multi-sided administrative assets.

3. Autonomy. How often have we experienced the teacher who is compelled to "balk" at doing what the crowd is doing, even though the majority represents a good idea, practice, or belief. Such a teacher needs to be "different." It is their unsatisfied desire for independence and self-actualization which forces them toward individualization. The need for autonomy is accented in a teacher because it is denied by the very nature and structure of the work. Every administrator should be aware that all people want to be able to come and go as desired, to say what they think about things, to be independent of others in making decisions, and to do things without regard to what others may think. But it's very difficult for a teacher to achieve any of the needs inherent in autonomy. The professional teacher must always do what is best for students. Teachers are in a "giving" rather than a "taking" profession. They are also in a profession which requires teamwork, cooperation, and consideration for the work of others. This fact does not diminish their need for autonomy, however. I believe this need is one of the incentives behind many negative teacher attitudes and practices today. This is one of the reasons teachers complain that they are being "treated like children." Because schools are highly structured, and must be, an administrator must be sensitive to fulfilling this need whenever possible and looking for other opportunities within the framework of the school to provide teachers with autonomy. Like it or not, teachers should not be bound by the same rules, regulations, and policies that govern students, for example. As students grow toward more responsible behavior, they are given more freedom. We need to be continually reminded that teachers are not students — they have already revealed that they are responsible enough to gain professional status in the adult world.

4. Exhibition. This is the need we all have to say clever and witty things, to have others notice and comment upon our appearance, and to say something "just to see" the effect our words have upon others. It's the need to exhibit that compels us to talk about personal achievements to anyone — at any time they will listen — even though we might be very boring or offensive. This desire is fairly easy to recognize, and it should be equally easy to fulfill. The problem is that we, as leaders, may be offended or irritated when those we lead reveal this need. That's why we sometimes choose to ignore them or "put them down." If this is the case, we are only inviting an aggressive retaliation.

5. Introspection. When we analyze our reasons and motivations for doing something and use the conclusions as a basis for understanding how others feel about similar problems and situations, we are satisfying our need for introspection. Introspection causes us to judge people by "why" they act in a certain way rather than "what" they do. It compels us to predict others' behavior, to "second guess" a situation. We usually derive a great deal of personal satisfaction when this need is fulfilled; it makes us feel wise, intelligent, and knowledgeable regardless of the position we are in. This is the need that allows a custodian to feel that he knows more than the superintendent and derive great satisfaction from this belief. Unfortunately, the need for introspection can also get us into trouble as leaders. Introspection is the source of prejudgments. An abnormal dependence on second guessing can result in our becoming professional critics and never doers. Rather than participate, we may begin to stand back, watch others, and judge their efforts. Involvement and active participation are the keys that fulfill this need in a healthy and constructive manner.

6. Avoiding Confrontation. Fear is a big factor in the lives of most people. In many ways, I think fear actually dominates the lives of many people. Teachers are certainly no exception. They don't want problems; they desire to avoid any troublesome confrontation with colleagues and administrators, not to mention parents and students. This is one reason why some teachers will not discipline a student in the halls or cafeteria who is not in

their class. It is the reason why some teachers deny knowledge or involvement in any contested situation. Those teachers who will not be drawn into offering an opinion are attempting to avoid confrontation because they fear a confrontation. From another perspective, fear of confrontation may compel a teacher to be reticent about strong desires to make changes, thus inhibiting creativity. Desires to explore new teaching techniques, variations in the daily routine, or just trying out new fashions or hair styles may all be repressed in order to avoid any potential confrontation. A good leader will recognize these fears, and the desires that are a part of them, and use other basic needs as tools for motivation and fulfillment.

However, we should always remember that just because these teachers are quiet and withdrawn in school with colleagues and administrators does not mean they will not violate a confidence out of school. Sometimes, they are our biggest "talkers." This awareness should always be a part of our efforts to help staff members overcome their fears.

7. Sympathy. This is our need to help students, friends, and colleagues when they are in trouble. We've all witnessed teachers come to the aid of the student they have wanted "kicked out of school" once he has admitted the errors of his way or when everybody is "down" on him. This need stems from the "underdog" syndrome. Sympathy also causes us to treat others kindly and do favors for them, to show affection, and to want others to confide in us. This motive is of paramount importance to school administrators. Through this need, it is possible to help us "turn a teacher on" to helping kids. Likewise, the presence of this need should never let us forget that we, as administrators, do hold both the final power and the authority in a school. Regardless of the circumstances, if we "get on" somebody and they become the "underdog" in the minds of others, some will automatically rally to their side. That's a fact. This is true regardless of the circumstances. That's why many things in a school that involve people must remain private and never become public. People's inclination to give sympathy should remind us that confidentiality and privacy are leadership "musts"

when it involves the problems and deficiencies of staff members. All in a school are aware of who is and is not performing. A leader must never forget that public statements or private discussions regarding the deficiencies of certain teachers may change sympathies. Such action may also change loyalites.

8. Endurance. This is a very powerful motive among teachers and administrators alike. To many teachers, endurance is a synonym for good and successful effort. That's why some teachers will impose and even force endurance upon students. It is this need that compels people to keep at a job until it is finished, to sacrifice, to work hard at a task before taking on others, and to stick with a situation even though no apparent progress is being made. Teachers often punish students who do not demonstrate this need — even when they don't demonstrate it themselves. They may even regard it as a character deficiency. Leaders sometimes enforce endurance upon their staff members in the same way. The wise administrator understands that the **effort** of doing a job can be as important to people as completing the task. To ignore either the task or the endurance involved can leave the strongest need of some unfulfilled; even worse, a lack of recognition of people's endurance can be damaging to their self-concept, causing them to feel timid, insecure, and inferior. To many people, what proves their excellence is that others could not have endured what they did.

9. Heterosexuality. This is an important need in the life of people. Teachers are not the exception. Heterosexuality is our need to engage in activities with the opposite sex. It is our need to be in love with someone of the opposite sex and to be regarded as physically attractive by those of the opposite sex. There are many ways to be a beautiful person. There are also many positive and healthy ways a leader can show people they are regarded as one of them. Unfortunately, there are countless ways we show people that we do not consider them to be beautiful people. The respect we offer to those we lead by word and deed is one of the most important. How we act with them, how we look at them, how we welcome their

being with us, the sincerity of our compliments, and the enjoyment we reveal allow others to know that we regard them as attractive people.

I hope you realize that the Nine Priorities we have discussed in this chapter are by no means an exhaustive study. These Priorities, however, in addition to offering a fuller explanation of the implications of the Secondary Motives, should provide you with a very sound foundation for understanding what causes people to be the way they are, particularly in the educational environment you are responsible for.

It is also very necessary to realize, however, that although both the Primary and Secondary Motives and the Nine Priorities help us to understand ourselves and others more fully, they really do not stipulate **how** we should go about bringing people's wants and needs into balance — that is, **how** we can fulfill the needs of our staff members. The next and final chapter in Part One will be devoted to answering this question.

4

WHAT MOTIVATES PEOPLE TO FOLLOW LEADERSHIP

In this chapter, we will devote our attention to how to motivate people to fulfill our leadership directives and at the same time acquire a sense of personal fulfillment and self-satisfaction. The importance of these Seven Individual Motivators cannot be overemphasized. All of our expertise in understanding what causes people to be the way they are is of little practical value, unless we can take the needs of our staff members and actually fulfill them in the context of leadership directives. It is through these Seven Motivators that the perceptive leader applies his or her knowledge of human beings and makes both leading and being led a satisfying and rewarding experience.

1. Personal Gain. This is the strongest and most prevalent individual motive possessed by human beings. In any situation, one is almost sure to think or ask, "What do I get out of it?" or "What's in it for me?" This is called

the Primary Question, and it's one we all seem to ask consciously or subconsciously in all situations. It's also a question all teachers ask of their administrative leaders: "What is he or she doing to help me do a better job in the classroom?" If the answer is "Nothing," a leader is in trouble. Examples of this need revealed are: more money, more say, more help, more responsibility, more recognition, more freedom, more leisure or more of anything. This need is completely self-directed.

2. Prestige. People are motivated by what causes them to feel important or will enable them to win approval or recognition from others. As administrators, we see teachers striving to meet this need daily. The best examples are those teachers who are always telling you what good things they are doing. If you're perceptive, you realize they want you to respond and praise them. In fact, they may keep telling you "more" until you do. Never ignore these pleas and never forget to respond in a positive way by recognizing their accomplishments. Needless to say, to do so reluctantly is a mistake. When you get a chance as a leader to fulfill a personal need of one of your teachers — fill it.

3. Pleasure. When the prestige motive is combined with the need people have to achieve pleasure, motivation to accept leadership is enhanced. A leader would do well never to forget the leadership asset available in combining these two individual motivators. When the need for pleasure is not allowed, people will not trust a leader, for they believe you are taking credit for all accomplishments and are likely to feel "used." The needs for prestige and pleasure are evidenced in those teachers who want to serve on committees, ask to give reports, like to serve as hosts, enjoy decorating their room, and write stories for the local paper. From a leadership viewpoint, we often "allow" these people to achieve tasks, and then we destroy our efforts by failing to allow their need for pleasure to be met. That is a human as well as a leadership mistake. Allowing the need for pleasure to be met will double their contribution. It will also generate a more positive image of you as their administrator.

4. Imitation. This is a need people have to follow the crowd and do what the majority — or minority — are doing.

This need is a vital asset to leadership efforts and should be used often. If another school system is doing something successful and you want to try it, relate this fact. If a teacher is employing a successful teaching technique, utilizing equipment in a unique way, or handling discipline problems effectively — utilize their success and stimulate others via the imitation motivator. It's called third-person support. The use of third-person support is a valuable instrument to reinforce leadership decisions, urgings, and teaching. The leaders in industry use third-person supports at every opportunity. In many ways, third-person supports allow one never to lead alone. Third-person supports not only say, "I'm not the only one who thinks this way," they also allow an administrator to open doors to new ideas as well as say things to a staff "through others" that may otherwise go unsaid.

The imitation need is strong among professional groups. It is evidenced in those teachers who belong to every professional organization, will vote with the majority, always "name drop" at every opportunity, or give the same grades as other teachers do, regardless of what the student earned. Another good example is that small group of teachers who always "stick together" on everything. From a leadership viewpoint, we should use imitation to stress the positive, reinforce good work, gain acceptance of a new idea someone else is using successfully, or get people to change their behavior. Third-person support is vital in leadership efforts. It allows us always to lead with the reinforcement of what others are doing successfully.

5. Security. This is a desire we all have for safety. It is revealed in many varied ways. As you will note, in one way or another it appears on every listing as both a need and motivation. Those teachers who never offer an idea or endorse one from another are simply acting out of a need for security. They are afraid of failure. Many people will not even offer an opinion when asked for fear of being wrong or offending someone. Never, under any circumstances, should a leader force the insecure individual to "take a stand" publicly. They will, without reservation, withdraw from you permanently. They simply cannot and will not allow themselves to be placed in such a fearful and insecure position.

47

6. Convenience. When a leader can combine the need for convenience with the need for personal gain, leadership acceptance and motivation are enhanced. Remember, we all want things better. We all want life to be a little easier. If a new proposal or suggested change is easy — we'll try. If it's hard, we may try, but we really don't want to. If we can avoid more work, we will. That's human behavior. We all know many teachers who will approve anything that does not involve them. We are all familiar with the teacher who would vote for anything which relieves him of some duty. The knowledgeable leader never reacts negatively to this need. Neither does he "explode" or express disappointment when people reveal the need for convenience. Rather, he realizes that management must adjust both thinking and action. If you can make something easy, never complicate it with an administrative order, policy, or procedure which makes it difficult — or appear difficult. Rather, make tasks and achievement easy, and leading will be easier too.

7. Desire to Avoid Fear. This need keeps revealing itself in every list, and it is a much stronger need than we will ever suspect. In many ways I think fear dominates and consumes the lives of many, many people. I think this need is among our most intense motivators. It stops people from even trying. A leader can never forget this reality. Fears dominate and control our thinking and lives more than we like to admit. Those teachers who refuse to be involved in anything outside their classroom or those who reject new concepts or shy away from colleagues and administrators often have only a desire to avoid fear. When we fail to face our problems, it is usually because we fear acknowledging that we have them.

These are the Seven Individual Motivators of perception and action which induce teachers to follow a leader. In the case of school administrators, understanding these motives must precede our evaluations of situations as well as our actions with those we lead. With understanding, one can readily adjust leadership behavior to get teachers to adjust their behavior. That's how we get others to follow our leadership.

NEEDS
WORK
IN BOTH DIRECTIONS

To lead people, you must study their wants, needs, and motivations on an individual basis. The perceptive leader is not misled by the outer projections of his staff. Neither is he foolish enough to "jump in" and disallow a need that should be met. He never talks to groups without understanding the make-up of the individuals within that group. He knows that individual thought governs group decision.

It's funny that we can put a man on the moon, but we often can't understand why a close friend, loved one, or colleague thinks and acts the way he does. Maybe it's because we haven't taken the time and given the objective thought to find out. Certainly the Primary and Secondary Motives, the Nine Priorities, and the Seven Individual Motivators contain the objective rationale for administrators to begin leading with understanding and direction. The needs show us how we are very much like those we lead; they also show us how we are not alike. They point out a fact which every leader must remember: the priorities of people vary. What may be a priority need to one individual may not be to another; what may be an administrative priority to us may not be to those we lead. But most of all, the needs should tell us that, if we are going to get all the work of the school accomplished, we must relate to many different wants and needs in many different ways.

Hopefully, every leader is quick to realize that use of the wants and needs is not a manipulation of those being led. Rather, it is the only effective way to get the work of the school done, while still providing satisfaction and growth opportunity for staff members. There is no greater priority for administrators than to provide the best possible education for students. It is the teaching staff that will make this objective either a myth or a reality. Yet, it is the quality of our leadership which will provide the climate and motivation necessary for teachers to reach this goal.

I venture to say that every leader could sit down right now with a list of their teachers and identify the needs that would characterize each of them individually as well as characterize the entire staff as a group. I wouldn't be surprised if the wants and needs, that we have discussed, didn't tell you exactly whom you should see privately before a faculty meeting, or immediately after a meeting, when a new idea, staff reprimand, or change in policy was to be presented. And may I suggest that you do exactly that. I suggest that you make out a personality guide for each staff member in your charge. Then, to get to know your new people, and better understand the old, here are some things you should observe, identify, and watch:

1. With whom will they associate and with whom will they not?
2. What do they talk about?
3. What do they avoid talking about?
4. What are they confident about; and with what are they insecure?

As a leader, always remember to act and react in a professional manner to what your people do. React professionally, not personally. Remember, in those Primary and Secondary Motives lie your own. Make sure you are not victimizing others or trying to satisfy your wants and needs at the expense of everything else. A school administrator can victimize teachers in countless ways. The shy always present an opportunity to show administrative power. Staff accomplishments may be your source of stolen personal status. Agreeing with a teacher may be your way of avoiding fear. A bad administrative decision may be the need for security revealed in an unhealthy manner. A new rule may make an organization need take precedence over student needs.

In addition, a leader may be asking, "What's in it for me?" That need within yourself may deny the delegation of staff authority and responsibility. A new rule may be initiated to gain staff approval rather than be in the best interest of students, or it may be made simply to make your tasks as an administrator more pleasurable or convenient. Never forget, you, as well as those you lead, are governed by the same wants and needs. The only difference is that the weight of authority lies with the appointed leader.

These facts add a special responsibility to being a school administrator. That is, they do if administration is a function rather than a position for you.

PART TWO

YOU AND
HUMAN MANAGEMENT

5

THE
MANAGEMENT
FOUNDATION

The human side of management is a social science. The study of Human Management can help us understand the best ways to go about achieving our goals when they involve the motivation of people — as well as coping with the problems arising out of leadership. If we are to profit from our study of the human side of management, we must approach it with an open and objective mind. At times we must form evaluations and judgments and arrive at conclusions, but they should be based on an objective analysis of the facts, not our subjective, personal opinions of people or situations.

The entire field of management can be considered as that branch of learning which deals with the ways to lead people and the ways people can be lead. From the broader view, management is concerned with the best possible ways for man to manage himself as a leader — as well as manage others — to gain maximum utility in the work achieved and satisfaction gained for both worker and leader.

It is an administrator's responsibility to get all the work of the school accomplished. Yet, both we and teachers must find satisfaction in getting that work accomplished, or leadership is always a continuous struggle.

The	**TWO**
Management	**MAJOR**
Foundation	**FACTS**

The study of management is based on two widely accepted, major facts. These facts are:

1. The wants of human beings are without limit.
2. The resources (human and material) available to satisfy the wants of human beings are limited.

The awareness and acceptance of these two major facts teach a leader many things about people. They also provide a certain "peace of mind" in leading and being a leader. When one is first approached with these two facts, he might say, "If that's the truth, why try? After all, I can't please people no matter what I do." In many ways, this is exactly the conclusion many leaders arrive at — and they quit. They also fail.

On the positive side, it is also these two facts that motivate all people to try to "get more" or to "get their share." That's why within these two facts lie both the management motivators and the management challenge.

The task of management is to make good choices. Our resources are limited in amount, but we must gain maximum benefit from both human and material resources. In this process we must understand that the wants of people are without limit — they always want more. If teachers earned $10,000, they would want $11,000. If they earned $15,000, they would want $16,000. If they earned $20,000, they would want $21,000. So would we! Wants, remember, are without limit. If a teacher received new chairs for his room, he would want new desks, and on and on and on. That's why we must make good choices — resources are limited. If we don't make good choices, our management skills are questioned.

All of these wants occur on the physical side of management. The real problems are on the human side. Here we must meet our responsibility as school administrators. Making good management decisions can best be realized by study, commitment, and application of the wants and needs of people and the Laws, Principles, and Theories of Management. Our study should be approached scientifically.

As we know, a science is concerned with the relationship between cause and effect. By this definition, administration can be considered a science because it uses:

1. Logical reasoning.
2. Observation.
3. And experiments through experience to solve problems and reach conclusions.

In management we deal with facts, hypotheses, theories, and laws and principles. In order to fully understand the meaning and implications of the Laws and Principles of Human Management, we must first define the terms that make-up these concepts.

1. Facts. A fact is a physical happening which our experience has consistently proven to be true. For example, it is a fact that if we do not replenish our bodies with food we will eventually starve to death. Likewise, it is a fact that fire burns or that we need a job to pay our bills. However, at one time, it was also a "fact" that the world was flat and that space travel was only possible in science fiction novels.
   a. Therefore, as administrators, it is essential to realize that what is an absolute fact to one person may not be to another. Often, facts are only relatively true.
   b. But this does not mean that facts are worthless or of uncertain value. Every field of learning is based upon a series of interrelated facts which form the foundation of that field. This is true in chemistry, physics, and in the social science of Human Management.

2. Hypotheses. A hypothesis is a logical formulation which attempts to establish one fact, or series of facts, as the cause of another fact, or series of facts. In practical terms, a hypothesis is really an "educated guess" at a causal relationship.
   a. We should realize that such a hypothesis may or may not be true.
   b. But that its correctness will only be finally established with the test of time and experience.

3. Theories. A theory is a hypothesis which has been proven as true, by testing under various conditions.
   a. Remember, a theory is more than just a "shot in the dark." Experience has proven it to be consistently true. A satisfactory cause-effect relationship has already been established.

b. Often, a number of theories will satisfy the same condition equally well. The truth of this fact encourages
constant reexamination in order to find a better alterna-
tive.

4. Laws and Principles. A theory becomes a law or principle after leading authorities have widely accepted the
truth and inevitability of the idea. Common examples
are the "Law of Gravity" and the "Law of Supply and
Demand."
   a. There is a significant difference between tacitly agreeing with the truth of a law and truly understanding how
   the law works in its full implications.
   b. Because the word "law" has the connotation of "being
   fixed," many people prefer to use the word "principle,"
   recognizing that our world continually changes and
   that new, more encompassing principles may be discov-
   ered.

When everyone, or most everyone, accepts a law or principle
for a long time, it may become a fact.

This completes the full cycle of investigation in the Scientific
Method. From this order, the Scientific Method of problem
solving has evolved. Let's apply this understanding to the social
science of Human Management by studying the Laws and
Principles of Human Management.

For the remainder of this chapter, I intend to develop fully
the four Fundamental Laws of Human Management which are
the very foundation of effective leadership. These four Laws
are "essentials" for your leadership program; any administrator
who attempts leadership without actively practicing these
Laws will most probably fail in his efforts, or at least be less
dynamic than he really could be. Consider these Laws closely,
and apply them to your own responsibility-situation.

THE
LAW
OF ORIGIN

Rationale: Institutions must operate in agreement with the reason for their origin and existence, or failure, rather than success, becomes the probability.

This is not an institutional theory. It is a law. It applies to business, families, churches, and schools. Without doubt, it is a management absolute in education. Failure to adhere to this law will get administrators in trouble with more people, more quickly, than any other thing they can do. It can result in the destruction of the individual as well as the institution.

In truth, administrative action which violates this law reflects an incompetency and obvious management misdirection that is, indeed, reason for termination. Little can or will be achieved in the presence of this inconsistency of direction and purpose. Quite the contrary. Constant personal and professional conflicts, a division of staff, and student and public unrest will be the ever-present school or system condition. That's the reality produced by a violation of the Law of Origin.

Management decision making that contradicts the Law of Origin is always without administrative defense. On the other hand, compliance with this law not only assures leadership direction, it also provides educators with the foundation and skills to make and defend decisions that are consistent with good educational and management practices. This law must be entrenched like a rock and practiced faithfully — for it is the foundation of our appointment to the professional position we hold as school administrators.

A
SCHOOL
MUST BE STUDENT-CENTERED

A school must be student-centered. This is a simple, yet all-encompassing fact inherent in the reason for the existence of schools and therefore inherent in the work of the school.

Everything we do in a school must be in the best interest of children. Schools were not created to employ teachers, psychiatrists, cooks, secretaries, custodians, counselors, or administrators. Schools were created to meet the needs of students.

Recent years have brought forth a new feeling among some educators. The school, they say, can't do everything. That may be true in a sense, but the school must be very careful in placing limits on what it will or will not do to meet the needs of students. When the school places limits on what it will do, it places limits on its effectiveness as well.

The school is a large part of every community. It is a focal point in the lives of parents as well as children. In truth, the school must be careful in making proclamations about what it will not do for those it was created to serve. Such action by any institution is the first step in bringing people to decide there is no need to support that institution.

As workers of the school, our competency as well as our security is totally and directly linked to how effectively the school can meet the educational needs of students. Any time we become teacher-centered or administrator-centered or centered in any direction other than that of student best interest, we have lost sight of the reason for our existence. That's a violation of the Law of Origin — and it's dangerous.

The Law of Origin operates on every level for every worker of the school — from the custodians to teachers to the board of education. There are many ways we can violate the Law of Origin. For instance, if we decide to clean classrooms at the time convenient for custodians rather than at the time of students' best interest, we are custodian-centered in this case. These kinds of decisions are not uncommon. Often, access to gyms, auditoriums, and classrooms is denied students because of the cleaning schedules of custodians. Make no mistake, this is a violation of the Law of Origin. True, it may be inconvenient and difficult to arrange schedules and get custodians to work at certain times in order to work around the needs of students. Yet, a school is either student-centered or it is not. Other examples of violations of this law can be seen when a film is not shown in a classroom because a projector would be difficult to locate and would have to be transported from another place, or activities are eliminated because a faculty sponsor cannot be found. Flexible scheduling is disallowed because teachers don't want it, or an assembly is not scheduled for fear teachers would be angered by the interruption. In all these instances, students' best interest has been overlooked or avoided for one reason or another. In each case, students' best interest has been placed in a position secondary to the wants and needs of someone else. That's a dangerous position for either a school or administrator to be in. These kinds of deviations can develop into big contradictions when one does not understand the full meaning of the Law of Origin.

When administrators violate this law by leaning in varied directions — for any reason — the position of the staff and the institution is jeopardized. Everything from administrator ability, to judgment, to credibility is subject to question and criticism. In truth, it should be. However, whatever we do, if we truly believe our actions to be in the best interest of students, our actions are at least defensible. Even when we error, if we can show that we believed our actions were in the best interest of students, we are in a defensible position. In most cases, I think you will find that our problems come when we do what may have been best for someone else — but wasn't in the best interest of students.

REFLECTED
IN
EVERY DECISION

Every administrator's leadership must be in agreement with the reason for the existence and origin of the institution. When it is not, the dying process begins.

This includes the establishment of the rules and regulations needed as day-to-day operation guides to the attitudes, philosophies, and methods used by the institution to fulfill the mission of its creation and existence.

It's not uncommon for educators to talk one direction and act another, especially when it applies to them. Of course, this is easily detected by students, teachers, and everyone else within the administrative and school orbit. Leaders may tell teachers to be student-centered when they ask them to do something — regardless of the extra work — then decide to refuse to allow a unit of study, offer an extra course, eliminate flexible scheduling or a student-centered service because it takes too much administrative time and would involve too much red tape.

These types of contradictions by administrators may begin causing staff doubts and spread to a general feeling of discontent. Such violations of the Law of Origin may culminate in leadership problems that move beyond solution. Remember, all administrator efforts must support and promote the fulfillment of the Law of Origin goal. Any deviation is a leadership mistake — one serious enough to bring about the destruction of an institution.

One may say, "We will always have schools." This is probably true. Yet, there is a difference between schools that are allowed to exist and ones which are encouraged by public support to flourish and grow. Remember, people may tolerate an institution when it loses sight of its purpose, but it will not support one to the degree that is required for it to prosper and thrive. Maybe this is one of the reasons schools always seem to face a financial dilemma. Never forget, the public cares not that the institution satisfies the wants and needs of the workers of that institution — unless the workers are fulfilling the needs of the people. That's a fact.

ADMINISTRATION ...
A FUNCTION

Practicing the Law of Origin facilitates administration being a function rather than a position. We see our role as leaders in perspective, and the direction of our leadership efforts is clear — not only to us but to those we lead. The Law of Origin facilitates the acceptance of administrative decisions, planning, and leadership more than any other management law.

On the other hand, if a leader is teacher-centered or administrator-centered, nothing the institution does seems to make any sense. Every administrative decision must be preceded by the question: "Is it good for students?" When all our decisions answer this question in agreement with the Law of Origin, everything from new programs to rules and regulations have purpose, direction, reason, and a common-sense foundation.

Too, it is the Law of Origin that gives educators, individually and collectively, a common objective. It gives all a base for decision making — be it a discipline problem or failing a student. It also gives us a system of checks and balances. Administrative orders, directives, and decisions are seen as facilitating the work of the school rather than hindering it. People are allowed to follow because leadership efforts make sense when they are in agreement with the reason for the existence of the institution. In truth, it is when we attempt to lead in contradiction to the Law of Origin that the majority of our problems begin. That's why the acceptance of this law is the first requirement of those who intend to lead. It must also be accepted by teachers, or they will fail to recognize the reason for their existence.

THE LAW
OF
TOTAL RESPONSIBILITY

Rationale: The Law of Total Responsibility relates that the administration is responsible for everything that happens within an institution. This principle applies to every level of appointed leadership.

It's a fact: A principal or superintendent is responsible for everything that happens in a school or system. Be it an individual school or the entire system, administrators are the ones looked to by the public, students, and teachers as accountable and responsible for all. If you doubt this truth, recall what happens when something goes wrong. Whether a boiler blows up, or a teacher mistreats a student, or a student throws an egg on a passing automobile — a principal or superintendent will be the one who gets the call. Worse, if the situation cannot be corrected or mended, the administration will receive the blame. These examples are offered to prove the point of a vitally important management principle. This management philosophy is called the Principle of Total Responsibility.

TOTALLY
RESPONSIBLE ...
FOR EVERYTHING

This management principle is all-inclusive. It relates that an appointed leader is responsible for everything that happens within an organization or the realm of leadership. Right or wrong, good or bad, fair or unfair — that's the way it is and that's the way it will always be. In truth, it can be no other way. The important thing is for every administrator to accept the reality of this responsibility from a positive and constructive point of view. This is the challenge and excitement inherent in administration. It is also the burden of appointed leadership.

Administration is not a place for the weak or those who cannot accept the authority that goes with total responsibility. The problem results for the individual administrator as well as the institution when the appointed leader cannot or will not accept this management principle. It is the failure to accept this principle that causes both a responsibility and performance breakdown within an organization. A stagnation of the people as well as the institution is the least result a failure to accept this management principle can produce. Regression is the most common effect. The ultimate result, of course, is the destruction of the institution itself. This is not an uncommon occurrence. Experience will reveal that destructions of entire organizations have resulted because total responsibility was not accepted by leadership for everything from finances to policy.

However, once the Principle of Total Responsibility is accepted, it changes a leader's entire viewpoint, perspective, and management approach. Remember, the point is that an appointed leader **is** responsible for everything. That's why the appointed leader is called an institution's chief executive officer.

A REQUIREMENT FOR PROBLEM SOLVING

When an institution is headed by administrators who do not practice this principle, direction is void for the leader as well as those being led. Most importantly, adhering to this management principle encourages and facilitates problem solving to be attempted rather than only to be recognized. Needless to say, it also results in problems being solved.

When administrators do not accept and adhere to this principle, problems may be identified, but they are usually allowed to lie in their place. This is true because nobody feels or is willing to accept responsibility for the problem or situation. Rather, we tend to adopt the practice of blaming others for a problem and absolve ourselves of all guilt and responsibility for any situation. Then, we voluntarily remove ourselves both mentally and physically from the leadership position to which we were appointed. Then, we can't deal with the problem or the work and mission of the institution for which we have leadership responsibility. We say, "Don't look at me; that's the math department's or the coach's fault;" or "The English Com-

*The
Management
Foundation*

mittee was supposed to get that done." The problem is that the difficulty remains.

When the person of lesser authority does not perform, responsibility for that failure always reverts upward — not downward. It never remains static. If a teacher is not doing the job in the classroom, it is the responsibility of the principal. If a principal is not accurately accounting for activity dollars, this becomes the responsibility of the superintendent — automatically. The leader who fails to assume a personal and professional attitude of responsibility for everything that happens within the school will never be a totally accepted leader. These leaders may be able to develop the skills which enable them to identify problems accurately, but they will never be problem solvers. Final responsibility always rests at the highest point in any organization, and unless this management philosophy is accepted, the Principle of Total Responsibility cannot be effected.

**ON
EVERY
LEVEL ...**

The Principle of Total Responsibility operates on every level. For example, students are responsible for their actions, yet the teacher is responsible for all things they do or do not do well. Likewise, teachers are responsible for their own ability, actions, and/or behavior. However, the department head is responsible too. The Principle of Total Responsibility always reverts to the top where, of course, the principal is responsible for all — students, teachers, department heads and the rest of the school team. The superintendent is responsible for everything that happens within the entire school system.

The Principle of Total Responsibility does not imply that responsibility and authority cannot and should not be delegated. Quite the contrary. It simply means that when anyone in a position of delegated responsibility fails to perform, the responsibility for that failure automatically reverts upward at that point. That's why the function of administration requires an appointed leader to accept and practice the Principle of Total Responsibility. When management fails in the acceptance, failures tend to become permanent. They must; for nobody ever corrects the situation. A department head doesn't call any meeting — so there is never a meeting. A teacher is failing too many students — and continues to fail more students.

AN
ALL-ENCOMPASSING
PRINCIPLE OF LEADERSHIP

The total responsibility concept is an extremely simple yet all-encompassing principle of management. When it is absent from leadership action, the person at the lowest responsibility level is usually blamed first for any failure. Worse, both the blame and problem are allowed to lie there because nobody at the higher level is willing to assume responsibility for the state of conditions existing. When this is the case, there is no leadership at all. This is the real problem. It is not uncommon.

However, when an administrator accepts and practices the Principle of Total Responsibility, control and a sense of responsibility are always maintained within an institution. Most importantly, control and responsibility can never be lost because responsibility always continues to revert in an upward movement. Loose ends are eliminated. True, teachers must be helped and encouraged to solve their own problems, for they too must understand and accept the total responsibility concept. Yet, if a teacher becomes stymied or falters for any reason, the responsibility for help or correction lies with the department head — then the principal. The problem is never left to exist or to be perpetuated. Whether it be a teacher having a problem with a specific student or a committee that has failed to report, the administrator must assume the management position of total responsibility. That is, we must if success is to be achieved. When this principle is not accepted by management, unfinished business and a void in the solution of problems become the rule of the day. When this happens, guess who receives the blame? You're right — the administrator. And that's exactly where the blame should lie — with the one responsible for everything that happens within the organization. That's a principle of management that applies to all leaders.

THE LAW OF TOP-DOWN MANAGEMENT

Rationale: Leadership is a management responsibility and should be effected from the top down in any organization.

Good management is probably the single most important item in the success and effectiveness of any institution. More than anything else — finances included — it is management that initiates and maintains the direction as well as the moral ethics of an institution. You can sustain an institution which is financially deprived. However, you cannot sustain one with poor management. Management, more than any other factor, determines the success or failure of an institution.

THE FOUNDATION OF ADMINISTRATION

Being a competent administrator is not an easy accomplishment. Without doubt, we can bestow a title and appoint a leader, but this does not mean that leadership has been effected. Unfortunately, some in leadership positions never truly realize the full meaning of this truth.

As difficult as achieving effective and competent leadership may be, its attainment is one of the most rewarding and satisfying experiences one can earn. However, this fullfillment can never be realized without meeting and relating to the challenges which are inherent in leadership. Such attitudes as, "I don't care what people say," or "That isn't my job," or "They will do it because I'm boss," never result in either individual fulfillment or organizational success. These attitudes simply reveal that someone who does not have the attitude, ability, or understanding required to learn to lead other human beings has been made an appointed leader.

The hard reality of leadership is that a person without a solid foundation of management beliefs is very unlikely to find professional success or personal satisfaction in a leadership position. Unfortunately, neither are those being led very likely to work to their potential or find professional happiness in their work. Too many leaders are prone to blame their followers for every woe. In truth, it is with the leader that the blame really lies. Every administrator simply must have a firm resolve in the Principle of Top-Down Management. This principle holds that leadership is a management responsibility that should be effected from the top down within the organization.

Many administrators experience continuous misery and frustration because they neither understand nor practice this principle. Quite frankly, some fail because they are confused by this principle. They believe that it conflicts with their beliefs regarding staff involvement. It does not. The Principle of Top-Down Management responsibility does not discourage staff involvement. However, it does fix responsibility for leadership rather than allow it to be disseminated to others.

GRASS ROOTS
IS THE RESULT OF GOOD LEADERSHIP

Many appointed leaders fail simply because they "wait and watch" as well as "confer continually" on everything and with everyone before initiating or offering administrative thought or direction — not to mention action — and can't understand why nothing happens or ever gets done within the organization. They expect ideas and plans to come from the staff always. They mistakenly believe that group suggestion is a prerequisite for staff acceptance. Hard as it is to convince some leaders, this is a management misconception.

Many good things come from within an organization and work their way to the top — as they should. Grass roots is a great source of ideas, opinion — and even responsibility. However, grass roots is the result of good leadership. It is not leadership itself — nor was it ever intended to be.

A leader may promote and encourage — but he must never expect or demand leadership for anything to come from within the organization. Leadership is a management responsibility. It is not the duty or responsibility of the teaching staff. Remember, leadership **may** come from within the organization — but it **must always** come from the top of one. In all institutions, be it a business, school, or church, leadership must come from where the authority is. With appointed authority and title comes responsibility — by ethics as well as by law. This is the function of administration.

When grass roots is the expected source of all leadership, then management becomes a position rather than a function. In truth, in institutions where leadership is effected primarily through grass roots efforts, those being led know it. All too often, to those they lead, administrators are regarded as an obstacle. Their position — from the viewpoint of the staff — is primarily one of noninvolvement, noncommitment, and nonaction. At best, administration becomes a position of unneeded liaison. In truth, these kinds of leaders are either unknowledgeable or fear the leadership role they hold. They also fear or fail to know and understand those they lead. Amazingly, these kinds of administrators are usually bewildered, hurt, and disappointed because teachers and superiors are critical of their leadership.

NOT
TRULY
DEMOCRATIC

Staff involvement is a benefit, a delight, and a leadership advantage. Although staff involvement is the desired condition, we must remember that the staff is not responsible for leadership. The administration is responsible for leadership in a school. Regardless of what one may think, democracy in running a school is only partial. Let's not think or pretend that a staff has more responsibility and authority than the administration does, or we'll find ourselves in more trouble than any leader can handle. That's the reality of authority within any organization. An administrator cannot delegate responsibility and authority where it cannot be granted. That's where many administrators get "in a bind." They put themselves there by pretending to be completely democratic when they can't be —

by reality as well as by law. Then, they can't get out when those being led want to make the decision they were told they could make.

It is simply impossible to be completely democratic and lead. Common sense should reveal that no one expects you to be. In truth, neither do they want you to be. Remember, consideration in making a decision is not a request to make the decision — unless an administrator has indicated by word, action, or lack of action that such a course was planned and promised intentionally. Democracy ends the first time an administrator must say, "No."

An administrator cannot delegate the leadership responsibility that is inherent in a principalship or superintendency to others. This is no more possible than it is for teachers to delegate the responsibilities inherent in teaching to students. If a teacher puts a student "in charge" and goes to the lounge for coffee and something happens, who is at fault? The student? I think not. If administrators pass their responsibilities to teachers and something happens, who is responsible?

The administrator who does not recognize that leadership is the function of administration is in trouble. One simply cannot fail to provide leadership in an institution and then rationalize away this void as a fault of the teaching staff. This is exactly what happens when the Principle of Top-Down Management is ignored, or forgotten, or rationalized away. We become "seekers of approval" rather than decision makers and expect every new idea, plan, or innovation to come from within the institution rather than the top — where the authority and responsibility is.

A true leader accepts and operates on the principle that leadership is a responsibility inherent in management. This leadership includes top-down management in every area of the work of the school. It includes leadership responsibility for the attitudes, philosophies, and skills of those in his charge. The Principle of Top-Down Management dictates that leadership assistance should come always from top down rather than be dependent on a process of filtering up from the bottom. When this is the case, the result is management being led rather than leading. Then, once again, administration becomes a position rather than a function.

THE
LAW
OF EVER-PRESENT LEADERSHIP

*Rationale: Whenever two or more people gather, leadership is
present. This resulting leadership may be a positive
or negative force in the lives of individuals as well
as the work of the institution.*

Many in authority positions ignore or overlook this overwhelmingly important leadership law. Some leaders feel that
their title alone denotes to everyone that they are the source of
leadership within a school or system. In many ways, this kind of
thinking can result in some vital management misconceptions,
especially if the appointed leader assumes there is no need for
one to establish and maintain his position within the group
being led. Such leaders are likely to believe that, when all else
fails, an administrative directive will cause others to follow
their leadership or correct any situation. If these administrators
would look more closely, they might see that titles which
denote positions of leadership, such as department head, team
leader, principal, or superintendent can sometimes be secondary and even insignificant positions of **actual** leadership in a
school.

TWO
KINDS
OF LEADERSHIP

Basically, there are only two kinds of leadership: appointed
and emerging. The **appointed** leader is the individual who has
the legal title, authority, and responsibility to effectively carry-
out the work of the institution he is serving. The principalship
or superintendency are prime examples for our discussion here.
However, when appointed leaders do not take charge of the
responsibilities inherent in their granted positions, leadership
will always **emerge** from the group that the appointed leader
should be directing. This is the Law of Ever-Present Leadership. The basic truth of this law is one that every leader must
remember when dealing with people.

The Principle of Ever-Present Leadership can result in a loss of appointed leadership which may be temporary or permanent in nature. In truth, whether the loss is permanent or not is determined to a great extent by the emerging leader. If the emerging leader has the desire to accept permanent leadership rather than follow the appointed leader, it is his for the taking. Fortunately, he may take leadership for one task or on one issue and then refuse the leadership imposed upon him by the group. On the other hand, he may become staff leader, not in title, but in reality. We've all seen administrators lose their leadership to a member or members of the teaching staff. That's the Law of Ever-Present Leadership revealed.

NEGATIVE IS THE PROBABILITY

Emerging leadership may be either positive or negative. Sometimes emerging leadership is good. Unfortunately, most often it is not. The reason negative rather than positive leadership most often emerges from a group is twofold.

First, people of equal rank are very unlikely to "speak out" against each other to defend a "nonacting" or absent appointed leader. This is not abnormal or disloyal staff behavior. It is simply the common way people react in the presence of their peers. An administrator must never discount the force of peer pressures. If one teacher is telling colleagues about "all the mistakes and wrongs that exist in a particular situation," or what teachers "shouldn't have to do," or "how incompetent the superintendent is," it is very unlikely that even those teachers who usually support the administrator, for instance, would say anything. They may not join the negative discussion and participate, but neither are they likely to disagree or correct the thinking of a colleague and defend the administrator. True, they may. However, their stance is more likely to be silence. They may be angered. But to speak out in support of the administration and against a colleague in the presence of peer pressure is the exception rather than the rule. If you think not, you haven't heard all the talk. On the other hand, an administrator should not be angered or disappointed when such events take place. This is simply people reacting in a human way.

Secondly, negative leadership emerges most often because the people who gain authority within a group — without a corresponding degree of accountable responsibility to some authority — are most likely to act and react out of self-interest rather than in the best interest of those the institution serves. This is exactly what happens in many teacher lounge discussions that end in criticisms approaching insubordination.

Examples of emerging leadership in schools are countless. An emerging leader simply "takes" or is "given" leadership. After gaining the authority and power granted by the group, the emerging leader usually proceeds in the misguided direction of self-interest or teacher-interest rather than student and school interest.

In many instances, it is through emerging leadership that many teachers begin to accept teacher-centered rather than student-centered attitudes and practices. A negative leader simply has emerged from the group and begins feeding colleagues negative thoughts.

**THEY
MAY
MEAN WELL ...**

Don't be misled; this negative emerging leader may be well-meaning. He truly may not be fully aware of the discord he brings. Too, he may be "pushed" or "forced" into a leadership role by his colleagues. I have always wondered, "If this outspoken and misdirected emerging leader were suddenly made principal, would he say those same things in the same way to colleagues at the faculty meeting tomorrow?" I think not. Why? Because once one is made an appointed leader, accountable responsibility has been added to authority. This fact changes the entire situation.

Without reservation, the best administrative counteraction to decrease the power and effectiveness of negative emerging leadership is for appointed leaders to meet their leadership responsibilities. Please note that I said "negative emerging leadership," for we are constantly striving to encourage the emergence of positive teacher-leaders within our staffs. We could not operate without them. However, the chance of positive emerging leadership developing without positive appointed leadership is slim.

**A
POWERFUL
FORCE**

A leader must never ignore or discount emerging leadership. Its force can be overwhelming. Without reservation, the intention of management is to have appointed leaders — lead. If they do not, those in higher positions of authority must correct the situation or look for new and effective leaders. If they do not, they and the entire institution will always operate at the mercy of emerging leaders. If an administrator adheres to the Principle of Total Responsibility — he must take this course of action.

When an administrator can accept the Principle of Ever-Present Leadership, he immediately realizes that an appointed leader must make decisions and take action. You can't sit on your hands and be an accepted or competent appointed leader. Too, a leader must know that continuous communication with every member of the school team is an absolute necessity if the presence of appointed leadership is to be effective. In truth, one must realize that being granted a position as an appointed leader is no more than being given an open-ended opportunity to prove that the right appointment was made or not made. No guarantees come with the appointment.

Respect cannot be granted by an administrative appointment or title. One must work continually at earning leadership acknowledgement and respect. Certainly, respect is not something that an administrator can demand, force, or insist upon. It must be earned.

None of us were always appointed leaders. Our experience should tell us that leadership acceptance and respect can be achieved best by leadership example as well as by providing tangible evidence of help, direction, and assistance to those we lead. Unless an appointed leader is willing to be an example of good leadership by word as well as deed, it cannot be earned. Remember, I said word and deed. The leader who does not actively provide those being led with the physical tools as well as the human skills they need to find success in their work will not find administrative success. One of the primary functions of being a school administrator is to facilitate the work of the classroom teacher. This is not accomplished by simply providing the physical things teachers need such as books, paper, chalk and other materials. This cannot be effected if teachers

73

can look only to each other for decision-making or help in meeting their challenges and responsibilities.

Never forget, we all ask the same question of our leaders: "What are they doing for me?" If the answer is, "Nothing," then those being led will look somewhere else for assistance as well as leadership. This is true for administrators as well as teachers. A principal looks to the superintendent and says, "What is he doing for me personally — to help me be a better principal and find happiness in the process?" Teachers ask the same question about principals and superintendents. Students ask the same question of their teachers. It's as personal as that. If the answer is, "Nothing" — then people look elsewhere for leadership. That's the Law of Ever-Present Leadership revealed. That's why an administrator can never forget the Principle of Ever-Present Leadership. If he does, he can lose the principalship or superintendency in more ways than one. Worse, everyone will know it — including him.

6

THE
LAWS
AND
PRINCIPLES
OF
SELF-
MANAGEMENT

As important and essential as the Four Fundamental Laws of Human Management are to leadership success, we must realize that, as administrators, it is equally important that we begin to look closely and honestly at ourselves as managers. Surely, no leadership program that is intended to be humanly oriented could ever be effective until we, as the responsible parties, clearly understand our intentions and motivations for our administrative actions.

This chapter considers exclusively the Six Laws and Principles of Self-Management as they relate to school administrators. The function of these Principles is to help us, as administrators, discover how to understand ourselves and our motivations more clearly in relationship to our responsibility positions.

*The
Laws
and
Principles
of
Self-
Management*

THE
LAW
OF MANAGEMENT SURVIVAL

*Rationale: This law of management relates that the most con-
sistent survivors in leadership positions deal honestly and sincerely with those they lead.*

It's a leader's normal, human concern to be directed toward
self and survival of self. Survival is an integral part of every
person's psyche. Those who become leaders are not the exception. Yet, self-preservation may cause a leader to act contrary to
the teachings of this management law. The fewer management
and leadership skills an administrator possesses, the more vulnerable he is to fall into a trap and to violate the Law of
Management Survival.

Leaders may tend to deviate from the truth in some way in
stress situations. This is especially true when we err and know
the fault lies with us. Nobody likes to be wrong, much less
admit it when he is. If the question of individual survival is the
issue, whether real or imaginary, real mistakes can be made by
a leader. We can even attempt to serve as judge and jury of our
own thinking, behavior, and mistakes — then rationalize our
actions away as "necessary" or "the only thing we could do."
We might even prejudge what the penalty would be if we had
to tell the truth. Then, we can permit ourselves to lie and skirt
the truth — and live with ourselves in the process. It's called
self-preservation. It's a common administrative reaction. But
it's not a good or healthy one.

Unfortunately, the older you get, the stronger and more
dominant this need for self-preservation and survival can become. It can govern your every communication, decision, and
action. It can be the most powerful, negative force in your
professional life — the need to survive.

Often, young teachers and administrators say that they can
make their own security. If worst comes to worst, they say, they
can and will change jobs. There is no apparent fear of hesita-
tion accompanied by this proclamation. I've had older colleagues tell me, "That's the way I talked twenty years ago too.
I'll be anxious to hear you twenty years from now." Yet, even
these proclamations from the young are only a rationalization,
and, in truth, fear is being expressed. The older are simply
more honest and too experienced to fool themselves. They

realize that they can't change jobs readily, and they acknowledge the investment they have made in the present position. They don't want to lose it.

Basically, all people are afraid of failure — regardless of their age. In a leader this fear of failure may be intensified. Maybe it's because a leader feels he or she has a set of critics standing around waiting to point out his or her failures. This reality has caused many leaders to think the only way not to fail or reveal failure is to remain totally and obviously in command. A distinct separation, they believe, will prevent others from seeing their faults. Even creating a kind of superiority helps, they think. Total command is their goal. They believe any means justifies the achievement of this end. When this is our thinking as administrators, fear is our motivator and secrecy is our communication. This is not an unusual administrative belief. In truth, it is quite common. Unfortunately, this common response can produce our failure.

An administrator should never forget two important facts.

TWO
IMPORTANT FACTS

Security is a basic human motive. People are basically insecure. Compound these two facts with the realization that we, as leaders, know we are in charge and with an intellect which tells us that we don't know all the answers — and trouble can be the result.

As administrators, no matter how we act, we don't know all the answers. The question is: Why does something within us make us believe we should always know the answer? If all the administrators could come to the realization that they don't know all and nobody expects them to — they might be able to better act out of truth with themselves as well as those they lead. It's the pure struggle for survival that makes a leader attempt to gain personal security through:

a.   Putting others down.
b.   Displaying one-upmanship.
c.   Attempting to build his own private building dynasties.
d.   Withholding information.
e.   Withholding authority when delegating responsibilities.
f.   Offering misinformation.
g.   Creating a false superiority.

The
Laws
and
Principles
of
Self-
Management

SURVIVAL
CAN
GET IN YOUR WAY

Administrators do these things for self-preservation. Yet, each of these actions of fear places our survival in more jeopardy. Hopefully, we realize that the greater our leadership skills and confidence, the less we are likely to contradict this law. The greater our skills, the less likely we are to be dominated by acting in violation to the Law of Survival. However, we can never forget this management law, for it reminds us that one of a leader's primary concerns is with self and survival of that self. If you forget, your actions can be self-deceiving — and the survival need can result in your not surviving.

Survival as a leader depends upon influencing and controlling your environment in a healthy and positive way. This control is dependent upon two things. It depends upon your image of achievement in the eyes of those you lead. Secondly, it is dependent upon your success in avoiding self-perpetuated conflict with those you lead by what you say and what you do. Truth is your best course for self-survival.

The Law of Management Survival relates that the most consistent leadership survivors always tell the truth and deal sincerely with those they lead. A movement in the opposite direction by management greatly increases the probability of conflict and failure. Truth cannot be continually suppressed. Once revealed, an untruth is both a personal and professional insult to those being led. It results in one of the biggest administrative problems of all — the credibility gap. Credibility gaps spread internally and externally quicker than most management diseases. People are likely to believe that if you lie or misrepresent to one, you will with all. That assumption is usually correct. Once established, credibility gaps are one of the most difficult obstacles for a leader to overcome. Unfortunately, without full disclosure of past actions, only time and truth can reestablish credibility and confidence in leadership. Usually failure and termination are likely to occur before leadership credibility can be reestablished.

THE
LAW
OF WHOLE TRUTH

*Rationale: This law relates that those in management posi-
tions who have difficulty relating whole or total
truths do so out of unsubstantiated fear. This fear
results in a leadership behavior that causes staff
distrust of all management communication and
may result in a loss of staff confidence.*

In many ways, we humans are afraid of truth. Most certainly, we are afraid of the whole truth. This must be so, for so
often we get ourselves "into a bind" and cause others considerable turmoil simply because we didn't tell it as it was —
exactly. The question is: Why?

Why can't we say one person told us about something rather
than indicate everybody did — or that one or two are unhappy
about a situation rather than say everyone is mad? Whatever
we call them, these kinds of exaggerations and distortions breed
distrust and cause many staff anxieties. And if we gain a
reputation for telling half-truths to teachers, they may not
believe our truths.

It's a fact: people want what they say to seem important.
Management is not the exception. Maybe that's why we tell
half-truths, for half-truths are often exaggerations. An exagger-
ation almost always offers more impact. Yet, the truth of most
situations will surface eventually. We know that. If this is so,
then it would seem to be a management need, for importance
and recognition may outweigh our logic. Most certainly, we
must be aware that a need for recognition may get in the way
of our truthful communication with those being led.

There is another facet of our failure to tell it straight that
deserves consideration. This is when known facts are purposely
omitted. People tell only part of a story — knowing all the time
that the whole story provides answers, while the partial one
only causes disturbing questions to arise. What moves people to
do this? Do they enjoy seeing others upset, or is this another
case of their wanting to say something important and allowing
recognition to get in the way of truth? Then, of course, there
are people who don't tell the truth at all. They change the facts.
This, of course, is the full circle of a half-truth.

The
Laws
and
Principles
of
Self-
Management

TWO
CAUSES . . .
DEFINED

Without doubt, a half-truth is often used to absolve ourselves of involvement in mistakes. Here, we can say, "He did," rather than, "I did," and deny our participation. Also, a half-truth can serve as an opportunity to bestow more credit upon ourselves than is due. And sometimes we tell half-truths to protect others. We simply don't think others can handle the truth. Although some of this is pure protection on our part, much of it results from a fear that the whole truth may create unnecessary turmoil. All are underestimations of the capabilities of human beings. Administrators are vulnerable to this type of thinking — and this kind of mistake.

It is not uncommon for leaders to use half-truths as motivational devices. If a staff needs reprimanding for being lax in hall discipline, greater emphasis may result if teachers are told other colleagues or parents are complaining. In truth, this half-truth allows us an excuse to criticize as a third person, for we alone have not reprimanded a staff; colleagues and parents have. For the same reasons, we may say that it is the board of education or superintendent who has instituted a rule, when, in truth, they have not. People involve higher authorities in half-truths thinking it may prompt immediate action, whereas reluctance might follow their request. Kids do it. Teachers do it. Administrators do it.

Without doubt, sometimes we tell half-truths because we fear the truth would make someone angry. We may tell a teacher he "acted wisely" in a situation — when in fact we believe he did not. We may say something has "been ordered" when the requisition has not yet been sent. When the truth surfaces, more anger may be revealed because of this deception.

All of these failures to tell it straight handicap the individual teacher as well as the entire school team. Truth is the foundation of teamwork. When it is absent, distrust and doubt replace confidence. That's significant. Confidence is the cornerstone for man's working and living relationship with each other.

It is not truth that people cannot handle. It's the deception of the half-truth that presents us with human relationship problems that move beyond our control. Even when truth arouses anger, the best course has been chosen. Time and again this fact is proven when better understandings follow this initial reaction. Truth promotes the formation of professional and human relationships which are prepared to meet tests and crises. This is not so with half-truths.

Imposing a half-truth is an insult. It says, "I don't think you are worthy or intelligent enough to be confronted with truth." It offers others nothing — except maybe a choice between ignoring your insult or confronting you with your lie. It is not easy to confront the boss. But it is easy to distrust and resent him.

The opposite is the reality of truth — for truth almost always brings people closer together than do half-truths. Only truth presents an opportunity for both involvement and meaningful action. Both are educational necessities. That's why it's important that an administrator tell it straight — the first time through.

*The
Laws
and
Principles
of
Self-
Management*

THE
FALLACY
OF STANDARDIZED PROCEDURE

*Fallacy: When management establishes standard operating
procedures for all tasks and assignments, success is
facilitated. Therefore, standard operating procedures
should be established for all projects and reponsibili-
ties.*

Not true. I just wanted to insert this fallacy into the Laws and
Principles of Management because many administrators are
not aware of the existence of the Fallacy of Standardized
Procedure. In fact, many strive to create a standard procedure
for everything and everyone. Too, many teachers push administrators to have such guidelines. There are many reasons for
the reality.

School administrators are usually good organizers. We are
planners. We like guidelines because we are leaders of large
groups of people doing a wide variety of tasks. That's why we
are prone to favor standard operating procedures and apply
them to the work of all committees.

Standard operating procedures do promote staff understanding and facilitate job completion, control, and reporting. However, all administrative procedures and guidelines should promote accomplishment and facilitate the decision-making process. That's why the fallacy of standard procedure should be
understood by all leaders. Standard operating procedures can
hinder leadership. In truth, the less the need to comply with
standardized operating procedures while making major decisions, the greater the number of sound decisions will be made.

There are many different kinds of individuals with a wide
variety of talents in education. Our profession is made up of
many dedicated, strong-willed, and highly educated people in
specific interest and learning areas. These people know their
area of influence and have a high degree of need for involvement within their area of concentration. These kinds of people
usually rise to challenges if this is permitted by management.
Standard operating procedure can limit productivity, curtail
motivation, and hinder the decision-making process. Every
school administrator must be aware of this reality.

Our staff is our greatest administrative asset. However, the
degree of involvement allowed by a staff is the total responsi-

bility of those administrators who make the guidelines for operating the schools. It is also the administration which sets the procedures of operating the institution. Yet, when standard operating procedure is a must, freedom is not permitted. Never forget, standard operating procedures force leaders to lower their standards to those of the group. It is easier and safer.

What standard procedure does for control, it does against initiative and creative thinking. Sometimes, when beginning a project it is better to begin within an open-endedness because of the limits inherent in standard procedure. It should be explained to those being led in this light. Then, at a certain point in the project when the plan becomes operational, standard operational procedure can be established.

The fallacy of standard operating procedure relates that specific guidelines should not always be employed by management to achieve maximum results. Rather, it implies that freedom should be encouraged at times — especially in the beginning or creative stages of a project. Standard operation procedure is best for routine tasks — not creative ones. A leader must never forget that guidelines can be established at any time. However, this fact should be communicated to the staff prior to their beginning a task or project.

*The
Laws
and
Principles
of
Self-
Management*

THE
LAW
OF MANAGEMENT'S MEASUREMENT OF
ACHIEVEMENT

Rationale: The primary goal of management must be improvement, for it is the only practical management goal.

So often, people gain leadership positions and then proceed to program themselves for leadership failure through the establishment of unrealistic and idealistic goals. Secondly, administrators have a tendency to target on one or two major areas and place all effort and emphasis on these objectives. When this is the case, a leader is apt to allocate all human resources to achieve excellence in only these one or two major areas. Likewise, a leader is likely to communicate such objectives with broad, sweeping statements which are neither clear nor understood. To one teacher, the objectives have one meaning, and to another they are different. Total misunderstanding results. This is a management mistake. When this administrative position is taken, a leader is likely to forget or deemphasize the total school or system picture which is the real management responsibility and must be our major concern.

THE
PRIMARY
GOAL

For example: An administrator may state that the primary goal for the current year is to upgrade teacher salaries. He might then proceed to tell all within the realm of the institution of this primary commitment — rather than reveal, for instance, that his goal is to improve teachers' salaries by ten percent. Never forget, the word upgrade can and will mean many different things to many people. It probably has as many different interpretations as you have teachers. A leader may think, for instance, that achieving a ten percent increase in teachers' salaries would be great and regarded as such by the staff. A leader might also think that the entire staff knew what was meant when the administration revealed a goal to upgrade teachers' salaries. When finalized, a leader may get a twelve percent increase for teachers, only to find that the majority were disappointed and considered the increase an insult and administrative efforts a failure. This is an example of the effect of not communicating goals as well as setting and communicating, by implication, idealistic but unrealistic goals. Many leaders do this type of thing often and create the image of failure when they have, in reality, succeeded. Examples are countless:

1. Setting the goal of getting all parents to attend PTA meetings. A realistic goal would be an increase over last year's attendance.
2. Announcing the goal of completely remodeling the Art, Music, and Physical Education Departments. A goal of making improvements in each department annually is the only possible achievement.
3. Proclaim that every staff member must be involved in an extraclass activity rather than increase staff involvement in school activities.

OUR GOAL IS IMPROVEMENT

Remember, the only practical and realistic management goal is improvement. However, the improvement goal must include progress in every facet of the school and school system operation. If total improvement in all areas is not the goal which administrators communicate to the staff, then we are promoting regression — which is fatal. Let me explain.

Special areas may be included in goals of management, but care must be taken in both effort extended and communication rendered to the rest of the staff. If certain areas receive the majority of the financial and human effort extended in a given year, an administrator may find some areas' goals realized while other areas deteriorate. Leaders may also find they are actively promoting the status quo and standing still in the majority of other areas. That's a management mistake. It is vital that an administrator look at everything within the realm of school and system responsibility in terms of improvement. It is a progression in all areas that produces excellence.

The
Laws
and
Principles
of
Self-
Management

A
VOID
PRODUCES COMMON PROBLEMS

When the Law of Management's Measurement of Achievement is violated, spotty management results. As we say, "brush fires" seem to flame up continually from many different areas we "forgot about" this year. Putting out these fires seems to take all our time — even the time we had planned to devote to the one or two major objectives for the year. Total management and total improvement must be the administrative concern and the administrative goal.

The paradoxical thing about not knowing about this management law is that it results in a management error that causes many leaders to move with great determination in the wrong direction. A leader may waste countless hours looking for one or two major objectives to present to the staff as challenges each year. So often, if a principal or superintendent can't find one or two major objectives, a sense of leadership failure is experienced. In many ways, that's probably the best thing that could have happened this year — for the leader, the institution, and those being led. That is, it is if one or two major objectives cause us to forget that the primary goal of management is improvement in every area. As we all know well, it's very easy to gain in one area and slip in many others.

THE
LAW
OF PLANNING

*Rationale: In achieving objectives, success is dependent upon the means, the tools, and the measurement of the plan which management establishes **prior** to beginning the task.*

In many ways, the less an administrator publicly discusses, exposes, or tells about a new idea, concept, or change before thorough thought and planning, the better off everyone would be. Too many good ideas get "shot down" before they should, simply because they arouse fears.

Before launching headfirst either into discussion of an idea or offering any plan to those being led, a leader must establish a plan which enhances success. Complete management thought and planning are prerequisites and must precede the public offering or announcement of any plan to the entire staff. In addition, it is a management responsibility to decide:

1. When the task should be finished.
2. Which people should be involved in the completion of the task.

PROGRAMMED
TO
FAIL

Much of our administrative strategy fails because we do not complete these two steps before initiating plans. Stated plainly, we simply offer too many plans to our staff "cold turkey" and proceed in the same way with the hope that success will result. Too often, it does not. When we proceed in such a manner, planning is void and management is nonexistent.

Planning is the function of management. Some aspects of planning are the responsibility of management, and if their responsibilities are not met, failure is likely to occur. Included in this responsibility are:

*The
Laws
and
Principles
of
Self-
Management*

1. Selection of tasks.
2. Establishing progress time tables.
3. Selection of personnel.
4. Establishing completion dates.

Without doubt, determining these structures and providing administrative guidelines and assistance facilitate success. Without administrative help, structure, and guidelines the chance of achieving success are handicapped. Mostly, administrators violate the teachings of this law because somewhere along the line they came to the conclusion that complete open-endedness was good management. It is not. It is no management at all.

Good management recognizes that "mental structure" on the part of the administration as well as premanagement planning facilitate immediate action toward reaching goals. Management must have "thought out" the plan — even though they may not reveal all the details of that plan to the group for fear it will limit creativity in the beginning.

Without administrative guidelines and direction, groups can leave an initial meeting where ideas are offered not even knowing what the proposal, idea, plan, or problem is — much less the direction they should go. Remember, loose ends scare people. Lack of preplanning threatens their security. If the staff asks questions during such meetings and are told "that hasn't been worked out yet," they worry even more. Worse, a faculty can leave such meetings feeling they have been charged to accept a challenge — but not having enough direction and leadership to even begin. Management must provide the structure needed to begin.

However, the objective of management is to allow an openness within the structure after the guidelines have been established. Remember, when introducing a plan, some structures can be the best aid to those who are assigned to complete a goal. It provides the framework necessary for achievement rather than "shotgun" efforts.

The best examples are revealed in sports. Golf has eighteen holes; football has lines and four quarters. The same is true with baseball, tennis, and basketball. It is the structure that permits the participants totally free movement within the framework of the game. Management's task is to provide such framework. It is the framework that allows maximum achievement. This is leadership. Without such guidelines, hours can be spent and people can walk away from meetings saying, "We didn't get one thing decided."

An administrator simply cannot present an idea without a plan. The major problems must be worked out and questions posed must be answered. Questions need answers before mass introduction, or the group is likely to fail before they have:

1. Defined the plan.
2. Agreed on the plan.
3. Decided who will accomplish the plan.
4. Established times for plan progress and completion.

ESTABLISHING PRIOR MEASUREMENTS

The establishment of prior measurements of goals as well as communicating the measurements of the proposed plan by management is vital. Without prior administrative measurements — anyone can evaluate the success of the plan at his own discretion and standards. That's significant to a leader because a successful plan can be deemed a failure if the objectives are not revealed. If you don't tell people what you expect to achieve, then the staff cannot say whether the plan is going well or not, is a success or failure. All this results simply because management did not reveal the level of expectation of a plan before beginning. Too, without establishing prior measurements and outlining the expectations of the plan to those being led, a leader cannot provide the incentives and rewards during the attainment of the plan. Rather, the leader can only praise following completion of the task when evaluation is made. That evaluation may come a long time after plan completion.

Every legitimate assignment given by the administration must contain a definable purpose and a practical measurement of progress which is visible to all. For example.

A. Assignment: Eliminate long cafeteria lines.
    Questions to be asked:

    1. How long are the lunch lines?
    2. How many students are standing in line?
    3. How long does it take to get served?

The
Laws
and
Principles
of
Self-
Management

4. How many lunch periods are there?
5. How many students are eating lunch?

B. Assignment: Get more parents to attend the next PTA meeting. Questions to be asked:

1. How many attended the last meeting?
2. How many parents attended last year?
3. How many parents could come?

The law of planning relates that the success of any plan is dependent upon the means, tools, and measurements that management establishes prior to beginning a task. When this law is violated, both the plan and the leader may experience constant criticism. A leader may be criticized for being disorganized, not knowing what he is doing, and not giving adequate help in achieving the goal. There's an old adage in teaching that administrators should apply as school teachers: tell them what you're going to teach them; teach them; tell them what you taught them.

THE
MYTH
OF THE PERFECT PLAN

*You
and
Human
Management*

*Rationale: No plan, regardless of how simple or complex, is
without imperfection.*

There simply isn't any doubt that plans are essential to any
achievement. From daily lesson plans to guides for curriculum
implementation, without plans our direction in schools are
scattered, at best.

We all realize that administrative plans affect the welfare of
students and staff alike. Careful initial preparation and thought
are necessities. It would be unfair to say that educators never
made the mistake of going off "half-cocked." As administrators, we have.

Maybe that's one reason teachers and administrators alike
are often suspicious of plans. Certainly, man seems always to
expect total success from his plans and is frustrated when they
fail. Too, we continually look for plans to be final, all-inclusive
and foolproof. We want plans with all the "bugs" worked out
— before instituting them. We want a perfect plan because we
think it ensures an ideal beginning and problem-free operation.
This desire gets us in trouble with the basic concepts of planning. Our desires for the perfection of the plan simply move us
beyond reality.

ALL
WITH
FLAWS

An administrator must never forget, regardless of how simple or complex, that no plan is perfect. All have flaws. In every
plan, there are holes. There isn't a plan that could be presented
by teacher or administrator that someone could not rip apart.
In fact, every plan could be criticized to the point where it
looked as if no planning at all had occurred. We can even shoot
holes in the people who made plans. This fact affects the
achievements of teacher and administrator alike.

91

The
Laws
and
Principles
of
Self-
Management

Whether it's planning the school calendar or developing a procedure for reporting tardiness, planning flaws can be found. If we're preparing a student handbook, working out class schedules, or developing a procedure for ordering supplies — something is wrong with the plan. It has to be — for no plan is totally perfect for everyone. Yet, if we reject every plan, we may operate without any. We may also ruin staff relationships in the process. We may find colleagues reluctant to present ideas. Worse, we may find it safe to refer everything to committees where time and energy is spent — then expose the flaws. In the meantime, nothing happens. While we wait for the perfect plan, nothing becomes our sole achievement.

OUR
BEST
EFFORT ... AT THIS TIME

A professional and realistic attitude toward plans is necessary before progress can occur. That's why all we can do is plan thoroughly and go with the best plan we can create at that particular point in time. The important thing is that we, as administrators, plan to the best of our ability and adopt the attitude that improvement will be made in the plan with time and experience. Then, we must communicate this fact to our teachers.

An administrator must recognize and teach others that a plan is a scheme of action — no more, no less. It is not permanent. It can be changed. It is meant to be improved. It can even be halted. Often, the Myth of the Perfect Plan prevents adoption or delays our beginning. It also results in our being unable to distinguish the critical from the trivial. We so fear "something will be accepted as it is" that we cannot focus on the larger goals during initial presentations. Indeed, a minor or insignificant aspect of the plan can capture the entire thinking of people. That's why a leader must adopt and teach a school faculty to practice a professional attitude toward plans. This management teaching must include a professional attitude toward plan acceptance, beginning, modification, and even termination. Management must think "major point" rather than "minor conflict," and get the entire staff to do the same.

Experience should teach administrators that without total staff support, the critics of any plan will usually be proven right. Likewise, total staff support seldom results in total failure. That's a fact of life in the success of plans. That's why total and complete staff communication is an absolute in initiating any plan. Part of that administrative communication must include an awareness that the plan is alterable.

The
Laws
and
Principles
of
Self-
Management

THE
PRINCIPLE
OF MANAGEMENT ADJUSTMENT

Rationale: To effect leadership, one must adjust his own be-
havior when attempting to get others to change
their behavior.

Many times appointed leaders believe that the higher one goes in rank, title, salary, and appointed position within an institution, the more subordinates must adjust to them. With this belief, of course, goes the attitude that the leader can and should be his own boss. One is likely to believe that's the way it is supposed to be. Any adjusting done should be done by others — not the boss. This belief is totally and completely false. Yet, many educators firmly believe that students should adjust to teachers, teachers to principals, principals to superintendents, etc. A close look will reveal that the opposite is true. That is, it is if one expects to lead other human beings. In truth, the higher one goes in title and position — the more he is required to adjust his behavior to get others to adjust theirs. That's the lesson taught by the Principle of Management Adjustment.

THE
PRIMARY
ADJUSTOR

The successful leader finds quickly it is he who must make adjustments to compensate for the strengths, weaknesses, beliefs, opinions, and skills of his people. It is only in using learned knowledge about human behavior and evaluating the skills of a staff — then making adjustments as management — that allows leadership to be effected. That's a fact. Management must always be the primary adjustor.

Every leader must learn quickly that in problem situations, it is the leader who must stop and evaluate the strengths and weaknesses of his people as well as himself — then adjust his methods and techniques to cope with both people and the situation. When this is not the leadership practice, problems may get defined, but they don't get solved.

When management does not make technical and behavioral adjustments, others are seldom motivated to achievement. It is the adjustment by management to the peculiarities, quirks, priorities, and behavior of others that allows management to change the behavior of those being led. The management attitude that "I'm the boss and that's the way it's going to be" only promotes fight or flight. It seldom stimulates or motivates those being led. Management is the professional leadership in our schools. It is an administrator's responsibility to utilize the methods and techniques which make people go in the desired direction. This can only be achieved by administrative adjustment. This is both the challenge and the responsibility of management. If an administrator can't make adjustments in method, technique, and behavior to motivate people — with some measure of success — effective leadership will never be achieved.

AN
ENDLESS
NEED

When management cannot or will not make these adjustments, any problem solving is temporary — at best. The administrator who says, "We do it this way just because I'm the boss," finds out quickly that it doesn't work that way. It never will. That's the Adjustment Principle of Management revealed. To get people to do what we want them to do requires one prerequisite if success is even to be hoped for: we must adjust our methods, our techniques, our actions, and our behavior to get others to adjust theirs. The higher one goes in an organization, the more he must be willing to adjust. Likewise, the higher we go in rank, the greater skills we need for adjusting.

If something isn't getting done, we must adjust our methods to see that it does get done. If someone has a "bad attitude," we must adjust our approach to change that negative attitude to a positive one. At times, it may seem our need to adjust is endless. It is. That's why a school needs administrators. It's also the

The
Laws
and
Principles
of
Self-
Management

reason we have been chosen as leaders. We are supposed to have the skill, self-concept, and personality to lead. We are supposed to have the ability to adapt to leading others to accomplish the work of the school. If we think of ourselves as the primary adjustors in all situations, we have the foundation tools needed for leadership. If we don't, both we and those we lead do not have a leader. They only have a boss. There is a significant difference.

CHAPTER

7

THE
LAWS
AND
PRINCIPLES
OF
PEOPLE
MANAGEMENT

This final chapter on Laws and Principles concerns the third
and equally significant aspect of Human Management: the
management of people. An understanding of the Twelve Principles and Theories of People Management provide us, as administrators, with a practical basis for motivating all of our staff
to function harmoniously out of sound educational practices
which hold the well-being of students as the fundamental value
in accomplishing the work of the school. Consider these Principles relative to your own staff and your own school environment.

*The
Laws
and
Principles
of
People
Management*

THE
LAW
OF REAL VALUE

*Rationale: People are always more important to situations
and achievement than are things.*

In meeting the responsibilities of administration and accomplishing the work of any institution, people are always the vital element in the leadership plan and the scheme of things. Because it's a materialistic world, the wants and needs of material things as expressed to us by those we lead can easily point us in the wrong direction as leaders. However, a close look will prove to every administrator that "things" don't cause problems; people do. "Things" are not difficult to manage — people are.

Things can rarely cause an administrator problems of their own volition. Material things do not have the ability to get angry, criticize, hate, plot, scheme, cheat, or act. But people do — and people will.

An administrator must never forget that material things come and go. They get "used up" or "worn out." People stay. The majority of the things we use in schools today did not exist in 1900. But people, with their Primary and Secondary needs, have remained relatively unchanged.

It's true that the teacher turnover rate is high. Yet, teachers are replaced by other teachers. They are not the same persons — but they are people. Every administrator should remember this fact the next time they think their problems would be over if they could "get rid" of one or two teachers. People who leave will be replaced by other people — and these people will be more like than unlike the people who have left. That's why an administrator must never forget that people are always more significant in the leadership plan and accomplishing the work of the school than "things." That's why people are the real value in a school.

TECHNICAL
VS.
HUMAN HELP

In management situations, we are continually faced with the

decision of concentrating our efforts on either "things" or people. Sometimes the simple fact that things are much easier to manage dictates our direction as leaders. Yet, an administrator needs to remember that although things do not cause problems, neither do they accomplish the work of the school. People do.

A school or system can be wealthy or poor, but the quality of education will always be determined by people. The quality of education in your school or system is not determined by physical things. It is determined by people who make up the school team. The task as well as the reward in both teaching and administration is where the people are — not where the things are.

It's an economic law that human wants are without limit. It's also a law that the resources to satisfy human wants are limited. That means an administrator can never totally satisfy the material wants and needs of a staff. As soon as one teacher need is met, another arises. A teacher gets new books, then wants new desks. The room gets painted — and new tables are desired. This perplexes us. We say, "You just can't make teachers happy." No, with material things you can't satisfy people completely. Remember, wants are without limit. However, by improving the quality and quantity of your human relationships, you can give satisfaction to those being led. This is your primary task. The human side of administration will determine your success or failure in administration — both in your eyes and the eyes of those you lead. The Law of Real Value proves this to be a management truth.

*The
Laws
and
Principles
of
People
Management*

THE
LAW
OF THIRD PERSONALITY EMERGENCE

*Rationale: The union of administrators and teachers auto-
matically brings forth the emergence of a third
personality which may be a plus or minus in accomplishing the work of the school.*

There is a tremendous responsibility in being an administrator — more so, I think, than many of us realize at times. The
influence and power an administrator holds in the life of a
teacher are immeasurable — and should never be minimized.
The vast majority of this influence and power is reflected in
what I call the development of a third personality. Whenever
leaders and teachers meet, this personality is developed — in
one way or another. The results of this formulation are the very
essence of constructive or destructive leadership.

EITHER
GOOD
OR BAD

The third personality is that growth which results from the
administrator-teacher union. The outcome of this union is either good or bad. There is never any in-between. I say this
because if the relationship with a professional administrator
produces nothing for a teacher — certainly that result would
have to be regarded as bad too. This is a reality that must never
leave the mind of a leader.

Of course, third-personality development extends beyond
leaders. There is a third-personality development that is the
result of the teacher-child and child-parent relationship. Too,
we are all aware of the effect one child can have on another.
One particular student may be strengthened or weakened by a
friend. We all know children who act differently when they are
with certain friends. The same is true in adulthood. We have
seen a person "come into his own" after marriage. We have
seen the opposite effect too. This is what makes the development of the third personality through the administrator-teach-

er relationship so vitally important. As school leaders, we must assume that our association will always promote the positive, the strength side of the third personality. What an individual staff member cannot or may not be able to do alone, he can — when joined with an administrator. It is this union that makes each teacher able to realize his potential. That's why every leader must look upon his or her position as a function. The creation of a positive third personality in a school is the primary function of administration.

A
DRASTIC
EXAMPLE

Probaby the most drastic example of this electric eruption of a third personality can be found in what others have recorded about such feelings. For instance, while writing **In Cold Blood,** Truman Capote lived in Kansas for a considerable time, there learning to know two young men who slaughtered an entire family. He worked hard and long at trying to understand what went into their joint decision to commit such a shatteringly bizarre crime. Psychiatrists concluded that "Neither would have done it alone — together they created a third personality." There it is. Weakness met weakness and had its moment of violent spinoff through this third personality.

It happens all the time. Only the degree varies. Either weakness meets weakness or hidden strength emerges to meld with another strength. In either case, there is an explosion for good or bad, and educators see living examples of this every day throughout a career. Yet, administrators need to understand that they themselves cause a third personality — for good or bad. It is inherent in the administrator-teacher relationship. If we come to understand that such connections result in forming a third personality and that these are quite real — then we can have some control over their development. This is leading through understanding.

This means a leader must help to put this third personality to work positively and direct its energies into useful channels. However, there are many reasons why a leader may fail to help a teacher develop a positive third personality.

101

The
Laws
and
Principles
of
People
Management

For too long there has been an intentional, overt separation between administrators and teachers in the school situation. The teacher may begin to view an administrator **only** as an authoritarian. Unfortunately, in too many cases, so does the teacher's administrator.

Another reason this separation has occurred is because of the "role" many administrators think they must play with teachers. Many leaders have come to feel that they must always be right. Regardless of the situation, they believe they must have the questions as well as the answers, always. In essence, they portray the role of sole purveyor of knowledge and truth as well as the "best way" to do things. It is this side that creates a negative third personality in all they touch.

Mostly though, leaders fail to generate the development of a positive third personality from the teacher-administrator relationship because they are unaware of its existence or because they don't want to. Many don't feel responsibility for it — unless the teacher's personality or attitude conforms totally to theirs. There are a variety of reasons administrators shed their responsibility. Then they get all "hung up" with right and wrong rather than how to help a teacher's dormant strengths emerge. When this happens, they abandon their real influence and power as leaders. As leaders, an administrator must never forget that together the school team can do almost anything. Alone, nothing is most likely to be our achievement. The third personality that results from the administrator-teacher relationship — whether good or bad — is the measure of management. If it is good, great things can happen in a school. Almost anything is within the realm of possibility.

THE
LAW
OF POSITIVE REINFORCEMENT

Rationale: In the absence of positive reinforcement from ap-
pointed leaders, negative human attitudes and be-
haviors are most likely to emerge from the group
being led.

This is not only a management law. It's also a law of human
behavior. Unfortunately, the truth of this law is revealed often
in both our personal and professional lives. In a school, negative
staff members are overwhelmingly frustrating and depressing
for those who are not. Yet, if negative attitudes cannot be
changed — or at least neutralized by those who are positive —
the negative may emerge as the strongest force within the
institution. That's the Law of Positive Reinforcement.

THE
NEGATIVE
DOMINATES

Sometimes, I am amazed that competent, intelligent, and
positive teachers will sit in the teachers' lounge or a faculty
meeting and listen while others offer every possible "I can't,"
"What's wrong," or "How terrible teaching is," — without
even offering token resistance. Sometimes good teachers will
even pretend agreement rather than risk disagreement. Maybe
this is another example of the power of peer pressure revealed.
Negative teacher attitudes can be overwhelmingly stifling and
destructive in meeting the need of students, accomplishing the
work of the school, and effecting positive leadership in the
process. A leader simply must counter negativism with concrete help and positive reinforcement. Allowing the continu-
ation and perpetuation of negative attitudes to remain un-
checked has an influence on the entire staff.

Yet, an administrator needs to understand negativism as well
as those people who have a tendency to be negative. The wants
and needs discussed earlier provide valuable leadership in-

*The
Laws
and
Principles
of
People
Management*

sights. Being negative is not easy or satisfying. It is difficult and unrewarding to operate always out of the negative. It is so much easier to function out of the positive. It is difficult to operate negatively because being negative is self-defeating and self-degrading. It is a horrible experience. All negative people realize this truth. They are not happy people. Worse, they don't know what to do about it.

As leaders, we need to realize that being positive is vitally important to us as well as those we lead. We need to realize that being negative is against everything education stands for. For every negative we offer, we give nothing. On the other hand, out of every positive we propose, we have at least suggested a possible course of action. This is the base for the practicality as well as the professional need for the positive in the lives of educators.

The motivation, stimulation, and confidence needed to begin with a probability for success is impaired by the negative. People need positives — if for no other reason than to avoid being consumed by the certain depression and failure inherent in the negative. A leader must understand and be concerned about positives. They are a tremendous force in the lives of educators.

A
VITAL
NEED

The need for positives as teachers and administrators is a practical part of our everyday existence. For those we lead, positives play a vital role in the development of their professional mental health. Without positives, hopelessness replaces hope. None of us can live with any happiness, satisfaction, or peace of mind if hope is denied. Rather, we live oppressed by what we have not done or failed to try. A leader must recognize the fact that when we offer those being led a negative, in truth we offer more than absolutely nothing. We impose an added burden which our staff must overcome. That's why our lives as administrators have a practical need for positives, for teachers as well as ourselves. That's why the Law of Positive Reinforcement should receive our constant attention.

We need to remember that our leading is positive if we praise rather than condemn, suggest rather than tell, help rather than impose, and share rather than force. We must never foget, even for a moment, that we should always be the positive element in the school scene. We must know that unless given positive reinforcement, negative teacher attitudes will flourish and may consume all in the school, including students.

Establishing a positive climate is an administrative responsibility. We are the climate leaders in the school or system. The Law of Postive Reinforcement is a constant reminder that the negative will result unless we provide the impetus for the growth of the positive. If we don't, "nothing" will be the tone of the school and "nothing" will be our primary accomplishment.

The
Laws
and
Principles
of
People
Management

THE
LAW
OF LOYALTY

Rationale: There is a direct relationship between a person's loyalty to a leader and the degree to which that person sincerely believes he or she is appreciated by a leader.

The management beliefs some administrators hold regarding individual and staff loyalty are among the biggest management misconceptions of our time. Loyalty is not bought. It is not derived out of special privilege or granted favors. It is not the result of personal friendships. Loyalty is a benefit that is derived out of appreciation. That's why gaining the loyalty of every teacher, custodian, cook, secretary, and others on the staff is within the realm and possibility of administrative attainment.

MONEY,
FAVORS,
AND BENEFITS

Many leaders continue to believe that money, favors, working conditions, fringe benefits, privileges, and other material advantages, gains, and benefits are the things they must provide individuals to create and generate loyalty to the administration. They believe these are the things which will keep their people loyal, supportive, and appreciative — as well as prevent their leaving to take other positions elsewhere. Many administrators think that a void in these areas will cause teachers to be disloyal, dissatisfied, and to want to leave their present position. Not true. In fact, nothing could be further from the truth. Too, no misconception could possibly have motivated administrators to move so diligently in the wrong direction than this widely held myth.

Leaders who believe these falsehoods have never looked inward. They must think that everyone is different from them — because these are not the places where job satisfaction comes

from. This may come as a shock — but people don't work for
money. They work for appreciation. All research supports this
statement.

People are interested in money, yes. But money has nothing
to do with their loyalty. In addition, money has absolutely
nothing to do with the amount of work an individual under-
takes. Money has nothing to do with the amount of work one
accomplishes. But appreciation does. Think about that for a
moment.

Once a living wage is achieved and a person has gained some
practical security which he can see, financial things are cast
aside in terms of job satisfaction. That is, financial consideration receives secondary priority if sincere appreciation is present. Only when appreciation is void do money, benefits, privileges, and other such tangible things become a sought-after
substitute for appreciation. In truth, it has been the leadership
belief that loyalty comes from benefits that have supported and
promoted teacher movement to gain these benefits. Lack of
expressed appreciation has caused much of the gap that exists
between teacher and administrator today. Appreciation is the
primary factor that determines loyalty.

Even a more attractive job offer may be cast aside when one
feels sincerely appreciated. The difference between $8,000 and
$9,000 will be rationalized away by the appreciated employee
as a gain that would be "lost in the cost of moving." In truth,
pensions and insurance programs fulfill the security need, but
all studies reveal that few people actually believe that such
benefits will ever be used by them. They have more of a
prestige factor than a security benefit. A close look at yourself
will reveal that these things only become demands when appreciation is lacking. In many ways, they serve as a substitute for
appreciation.

THE
LEAST
SIGNIFICANT

Strangely enough, the least significant way of showing appreciation to a worker is via money. Of all things it is, money is

*The
Laws
and
Principles
of
People
Management*

not personal. It is not appreciation. When it is given, loyalty is not necessarily achieved.

We humans are strange creatures. When more money is given to us for the work we are doing, we are more likely to regard the increased wage as something we were "owed" and should have had a "long time ago." Yet, we persist in pushing for the wrong things as leaders and ignore or deny the leadership action which would make staff loyalty a reality. By our very own hand, we violate facilitating the Law of Loyalty continually. Then, we can't understand why we do not achieve our desires — such as gaining the loyalty of those we lead.

We all know children who have received all the money a parent could give them — but no personal understanding and attention. As educators, we all know and fully understand the results of such parent action too. We can't understand how parents could be so dumb. Yet, we can't transpose this personal knowledge to our profession when we work as leaders of others. We make the same mistakes over and over again in our attempts to gain loyalty.

**A
COMMON
BASE**

Love is recognition and recognition is love. Lack of appreciation can destroy love. Don't fool yourself for a moment that love is only personal. It is professional too. The real problems people face in their professional lives are the same ones they face in their personal lives. These problems are loneliness, neglect, mistreatment, lack of touch, lack of communication, lack of availability, and not feeling needed. All result in a loyalty void — both as givers and receivers. All the result of management failures. In many ways they are unforgivable management failures.

Revealing appreciation to people is not only an administrative responsibility. It is also an administrative opportunity. It is the opportunity to give recognition and bestow appreciation for a personal contribution as well as the acceptance of an individual's contribution. It creates administrative loyalty. Remember, loyalty is a two-way street.

Surely every administrator can realize that this is the primary reason behind promoting professionalism. Professionalism gives us **instant respect.** It puts a name and label on respect. That's a fact. This is also the reason for the value and importance of granting titles. Yet, neither will give loyalty. Administrative loyalty can only be achieved through demonstrating sincere appreciation to those being led for their accomplishments or for their "simply being." This is one of the primary functions of management. In truth, this law is as important to a leader both personally and professionally as it is to those being led. Here both win or both lose. The responsibility lies with management. If you want loyalty, you won't have it, and you can't get it without appreciation.

The
Laws
and
Principles
of
People
Management

PRINCIPLE
OF
PRIDE

Rationale: Once established by management, pride will result in greater individual and group accomplishment through self and peer pressure — without additional pressures or incentives from management.

Pride is the result of good leadership. However, it is perpetuated out of self-pressure — not administrative pressure. Once established, it only needs to be reinforced by administrative praise, appreciation, and acknowledgment. Management simply provides the environment and sets the tone which creates the probability of self-pressure development.

Ask yourself these questions to discover the truth inherent in this principle of management.

a. Why do some staff suggest having more activities for students?
b. Why do some teachers work at night planning, grading, and preparing lessons?
c. Why do teachers "fix up" the lounge?
d. Why do some volunteer for every group?
e. Why do some faculties move relentlessly towards excellence?
f. Why are some teachers always the first to school in the morning?
g. The last to leave?

Because of pride. A leader must recognize pride for what it is. Once established, pride is among a leader's best motivational tools. It operates when things are going well, and it operates when things are bad. It gets things done regardless of the odds, and it always unites for good. That's why every leader needs to use it.

ESTABLISHING
THE
CLIMATE

Unfortunately, in our society, we have different rules and

regulations we must follow when we're talking about things like pride. It's OK to have "pride" in our football teams. However, sometimes we go to great lengths to hide our pride because we feel it is a sign of vanity, is unmanly, a sign of weakness, or unfashionable. For instance, boys can't cry. Boys can't appear hurt either. As adults, we're supposed to endure "cuts" and "put downs" without saying a word or showing any emotion. We are taught, in fact, that we should not be motivated by pride in self — that such a behavior is too self-directed or conceited. Only the athletic world accepts pride for its true importance. Only the athletic world makes full use of the value of pride for both the individual and the group. As school administrators, we can learn much from our coaches.

Failure to understand pride is a foolish management error. Pride has deep and far-reaching implications. Pride is within us all. It governs our thinking and our behavior. As leaders, an individual's pride can never be denied if we expect that person to perform to his or her potential.

For instance, our failure to allow people to "save face" in certain situations and keep their "respect" causes management many problems. You can't put people in a box. You can't embarrass people by word, action, rule or regulation — and expect to survive as a leader. Such administrative behavior insults people and denies them their pride. To be oblivious to the fact that we often deny pride as leaders is an error of significant proportions.

How many times have you seen people "boil over" inside in many situations but say nothing — and then "explode" on other minor occasions. In truth, we often fail to see that the real cause of these kinds of explosions was another incident. Then, we try problem solving on the second issue and don't understand why we don't succeed. Pride was denied during the first incident. That's the real problem.

AN ADMINISTRATIVE ASSET

Every leader must be cognizant of the need people have for pride. We must make sure that we don't "win the battles" and

The
Laws
and
Principles
of
People
Management

"lose the war" because our treatment of people directly or indirectly denies them pride. Pride is something we must promote — not deny. It is our most positive self-perpetuating motivational tool for accomplishing the work of the school. Pride can't be achieved with pressure, orders, or directives. That's why a leader must be very careful not to deny people pride by the things he does. Sometimes, pride is denied without even realizing what is being done. We do this in many ways. For instance:

a. Don't tell people how to "act," dress, or behave. Many administrators destroy the climate for the development of pride by giving instructions prior to faculty meetings, making assignments in a dictatorial way, and poking fun at volunteers.

b. Talk about your truths — but don't impose them on others — share them. When you try to impose your truths upon others, you are telling those you lead that you think you are smarter than they are.

c. Don't get involved in the rights and prerogatives of others without invitation. Never forget, embarrassed kittens become tigers.

A leader must recognize that many human pride motivators are hard to detect because people have been taught to hide pride. People will even tell us they feel pride as a motivator is unimportant in their lives. We tend to believe them, and this leads us astray. It's a mistake for a leader to think these people are mature and possess more self-confidence when they tell us pride is not a factor in their lives. It is. Behaviors which reveal a need for pride include:

a. Fear of being left out.
b. Fear of rejection.
c. Fear of inadequacy.

These individual pride factors cause proud people not to participate rather than face the consequences of revealing their true feelings. To resolve a pride situation — make sure your own pride is not getting in the way of your leadership efforts.

Your teachers should be fiercely proud of you, students, their school, their system, and themselves. If they are, motivating your staff to accomplish the work of the school is among the easier things you do. If your staff is not proud of these things, you and your actions may be the primary reason the ball has not started its self-sustaining roll.

THE
LAW
OF TRUST

*Rationale: Trust is a necessary ingredient in the leader-follow-
er relationship which emerges from positive administrative input — not from special privilege,
title, or appointment — and requires a mutuality
of dependence.*

Teachers need to trust administrators. Likewise, administrators need to trust teachers — and very much need for teachers
to trust them. We have passed into a time in our society when a
word like trust has more practicality in the dictionary than in
real life, or so it seems. As much as one may hate to admit it,
placing trust in others is not regarded as the wise thing to do. In
fact, it may even be considered dumb. If this is not so, then the
lessons we are teaching each other as adults as well as the
instruction we are giving students in our schools today indicate
that this is the more accepted and practiced truth.

Trust nobody we say, maybe not even yourself. We teach
students this every day. Secure your school books as well as
your bicycle, always. Write your name in your clothes, mark
your books, label your gym clothes — not for easy recognition
and convenience — but to protect against the untrustworthy.
You can't even trust your neighbors. Everybody knows that.
The radio, newspaper, and television advise adults continually
to lock their cars so they won't "help a good boy go bad." I
hope every teacher and administrator fully realizes the significance of such reasoning. This kind of rationale, indeed, ex-
presses and reveals a need for a revitalization regarding the
basic qualities of human character. Otherwise, human existence is destined for a low quality of life. Without reservation,
it is this kind of thinking which has made leading more difficult in recent years. But that's not all.

PAST
THE
POINT OF DISTRUST

We have moved past the point of distrust and suspicion. This

The
Laws
and
Principles
of
People
Management

movement has clouded our perspective. It is not uncommon for people to label the victim of trust with the title of "dumb" or "stupid" after the attack. How many times have you heard parents and even teachers condemn the victim for being so foolish as to leave a locker unlocked or leave books in a class-room or cafeteria unattended? How many times have you seen understanding and assistance withdrawn or denied because the victim was so "stupid"? We even, at times, indicate someone deserved to have something stolen because of his "careless-ness."

As leaders, we need to take a close look at these attitudes which have emerged in our society. We need to talk about these attitudes with our staff — as well as our students. Trust is a necessary ingredient for teacher and administrator alike. Without doubt, trust must be on both sides, or the potential of both teacher and leader is diminished and may be rendered ineffective.

NOT
AUTOMATIC

Most certainly, if there is one thing that facilitates the work of the classroom teacher and his relationship with administra-tors, it is trust. Trust knocks down walls between teacher and leader. When teachers give complete and total trust to leaders, doors swing wide open. Hesitancy, reluctance, and caution are replaced by listening, eagerness, and involvement. When trust is absent, the beginning may never be allowed to occur.

Administrators often make the mistake of thinking that trust is something automatic that teachers should always give their leaders. If we feel this to be true, we may be counting on our separate and unique status as professional administrators to work to our benefit when it will not. If we insist on leaning on this as a foundation, it will surely collapse under us. Never forget, trust is built out of positive input — not out of special privilege or position.

We can't teach distrust to those we lead by the rules we make and the advice we give — and expect this distrust to stop at our door. It will not. Our administrative teachings, by word and deed, apply to us as well as others. We need to think very seriously about this fact as leaders. If ever a time existed to renew the moral characteristics of establishing and gaining the trust of those we lead, it is now.

Surely, we know that trust is not automatic. Neither is it always learned quickly. Yet, it is worth nurturing as well as waiting for — because a carefully structured foundation is not easily moved from its moorings. Throughout the entire process of nurturing, a leader must never forget that trust requires a mutuality of dependence. In truth, that is what trust is in the last analysis.

AN ABSOLUTE NECESSITY

An administrator must fully realize the need teachers have to trust — as well as be trusted. That's why we need to give special attention to trust and all of its ramifications in the life of a teacher. The leadership for its revitalization can begin with us, for trust must be shared between administrator and teacher. If not, a form of disintegration results. Nothing positive can result when there is distrust on either side. As administrators, the initiative for beginning this teaching lies with us. After all, we are the leaders of our schools.

The basic ingredient of trust is personal integrity. The leader who cannot trust himself shall never trust teachers. The foundation of all integrity and trust is the faith we have in our own integrity. Surely, we can openly pass trust to our teachers — even if we fear violations of that trust in the beginning. If we can't, then trust will never be on either side of the teacher-administrator relationship, and a leadership necessity will always be void.

*The
Laws
and
Principles
of
People
Management*

LAW
OF
EFFECTIVENESS

*Rationale: The success of any project or task is dependent
upon the quality of participation which is delegated by management.*

The work of the school is limitless. Sometimes it seems as if
there is more to do in a year than we can get done in a lifetime.
Every leader realizes that both responsibility and authority
must be delegated to others if tasks are to be completed. Yet,
"what" and "how much" and "who" should be given authority
and responsibility for various school responsibilites has always
been a big and difficult management question. Too, because
we are ultimately responsible for all, delegating has been a
special problem for administrators.

NOBODY
LIKE
ME

Without doubt, we all know that the administrator who tries
to "do it all" will achieve little. Yet, there's a little bit of the
belief that "nobody can do it as well as I" in us all — or so it
seems. And that may be true. It may be true in some instances
that a subordinate will not be able to accomplish a duty as
quickly and effectively as you can. But the real truth is that
unless authority and responsibility are delegated, the majority
of the educational priorities in a school or system will not be
started — much less accomplished. To fear delegating responsibility is not healthy thinking on the part of management. In
many ways, it is the result of an institution which is administration-centered.

This personal belief must be discarded if success is to be
achieved as a leader. Success in administration is only achieved
by getting others to share in the work of the school and helping
them enjoy every minute of it. The primary task of management is to:

116

a. Involve as many people as possible in various projects.
b. Assign the proper number of people to facilitate success of the project rather than understaff or overstaff so that everyone can be on a committee.
c. Involve as many as possible in something significant.
d. Pick the right people to serve in the right places.
e. Motivate and stimulate people in the direction we want them to go.
f. Give people responsibility and authority to complete a task.
g. Create an accountable situation.

Delegating is one of the biggest responsibilities of management. Achievement of the work of the school and the maximum utilization of personnel prove the competency and effectiveness of leadership. Remember, the most costly of all expenditures is people. No expenditure is more expensive to a school than the staff. Yet, human waste is the greatest resource waste of all. That's why the staff is both the greatest expense and the greatest asset of the institution.

Many leaders are not able to delegate. Some can't even force themselves to move in this direction. They can only delegate token authority and minor responsibilities. Usually, there are six reasons why some leaders cannot and will not delegate responsibilities. They do not delegate because it requires:

a. Sharing.
b. Instruction.
c. Giving up responsibility.
d. Giving up authority.
e. A change in attitude and feelings toward control.
f. A dependence upon others.

Yet, the Law of Effectiveness relates that the success of any project is dependent upon the quality of participation which is delegated by management. A leader can only motivate people by appealing to their Primary and Secondary needs. This does not mean we should make a "big deal" out of every assignment. Quite the contrary. A good leader tries to accomplish participation **without** making a big deal out of it. Remember, a big deal is pressure, not voluntary participation.

The
Laws
and
Principles
of
People
Management

THE
LAW
OF DOMINANCE

Rationale: Dominance is a destructive leadership characteristic that results when management makes itself appear superior by making others inferior.

Every leader wants to feel competent. All want to have a sense of control within an institution or system because they are responsible and accountable for all. Yet, there is a vast difference between control and dominance — and every leader needs to know the difference. When they do not, leaders are likely to create an attitude and climate that stifle the productivity of the staff and are destructive to both a leader and the institution.

DEFINED ...

Literally, **to dominate** means "to name under." This fact should give leaders a linguistic as well as psychological appreciation of the word. Obviously, for one substance to be "under," another must be above. Therefore, if a leader feels a need or desire to dominate, at least part of that desire comes from wanting to be over someone else. Unfortunately, when an administrator dominates the staff, he finds himself superior by finding others inferior. That's the ugly truth in domination.

Examples in life are countless. The misery of domination can be found anywhere. Husbands dominate wives and wives dominate husbands. Governments may dominate people and may even try to dominate other governments. The results are always the same. One attempts to gain the position of being over another. Usually superiority is achieved by proving others inferior. It is a sad reality, and little justification is gained from the fact that selfishness or insecurity or any other reason may be the force that propels the desire to dominate into a real-life reality.

From pure experience, I have found insecurity most often at fault. More often than not, the insecure leader will assume the mask of inordinate authoritarianism — or try to — with some

118

or all of the people in his life. In psychologically oriented circles, this is "old hat." As educators, as well as administrators, we should immediately recognize the insecurity found in domination. Recognition is not the only problem. The problem is that school administrators sometimes fail to practice those principles they have learned regarding dominance and healthy leadership. Sometimes, administrators get these principles confused when applying them to their jobs as leaders.

Facts are facts, and evidence assures us that insecurity can really exist even in the individual who seems and acts terribly secure — like a department head, principal, or superintendent. Unfortunately, those leaders who dominate are seldom competent and happy — even when their efforts appear successful. Their feelings of insecurity are ever-present and hound their every action, behavior, and decision. Insecurity even rules their appointments of subordinates as well as staff members.

THE
TRUEST
SYNONYM

Insecurity is a vague description of several very well-defined feelings or emotions. Perhaps the truest synonym for insecurity is "unacceptability." In truth, it is the conviction of self-unacceptability against which the insecure leader is struggling. This conviction is often expressed as a desire to dominate. As we well know, it is not uncommon to see a school administrator who is or feels unacceptable to those being led. We've all heard too that it's a lonely chair the administrator sits in. If it is, it's because the administrator has made it that way. But the fact remains that if a form of administrative dominance has been built, a staff will not be "drawn" to the leader. Dominance forces people away.

Perhaps history can furnish no worse example of dominance in leadership than a Machiavelli or a Hitler. These individuals built small empires out of the selfishness and insecurity which drove them to perfect their methods of dominating. On a lesser scale, the same type of domination occurs in homes as well as classrooms and administrative offices. Out of insecurity, people

*The
Laws
and
Principles
of
People
Management*

try to build their own little dynasties where absolute control is maintained by domination. The result is that superiority is gained out of making others inferior. When domination is characteristic of an administrator, plans, ideas, and motivation can be ruined by this one leadership behavior. Proving others inferior is not our mission. None can deny that some teachers can be ideal victims for the unscrupulous dominator. If we, as leaders, recognize our own need to dominate, we must deal with these feelings. If not, we teach teachers to operate in a like manner with students — out of their weaknesses rather than their strengths.

The Law of Dominance teaches us that it is a force that is almost never constructive and almost always destructive. The desire to dominate is strongest among those who have the least legitimate claim to power or adulation. Motivated by insecurity, they error in failing to realize that real power and authority can't be taken. It must be given. Those leaders cling to the belief that the world is a savage place where the weak perish and the strong survive. They overlook the fact that if this is so, it is because of their own savagery. Hopefully, a school leader is not the one from whom teachers and students alike learn to need either to be dominated or to dominate. Instead, administrators must help people learn to build human strengths, not nurture individual weaknesses.

The Law of Dominance tells us that the potential of a school staff will never be reached with the administrator who dominates. The law also tells us that eventually the dominator will succumb and not succeed over a long period of time. Hopefully, every school administrator realizes this is not the 1800's. Dominance in leadership is a technique of the past. It is gone. So are many of the leaders who used it.

LAW
OF
FILTERED INFORMATION

You
and
Human
Management

Rationale: The more power and influence possessed by a leader, the more the information received from those being led will be filtered.

The Law of Filtered Information relates that information received by a leader from subordinates is filtered either by omission of the facts or distortion, if the information desired reflects negatively upon the one providing the information. Generally speaking, this is true because subordinates can rationalize away their actions and beliefs out of self-preservation. When people are dealing with the boss, it is likely that they will act out of three conscious or subconscious beliefs:

1. It is not their responsiblity to tell you things that would cause their judgment, competency, or actions to be revealed in an unfavorable light. That does not mean they will lie. It simply means they may omit some very important facts you might need to know.
2. You are the higher authority, and it is automatically assumed by subordinates that you have more information than they do. Therefore, they can and will assume they are only providing "a part" of the information you need or are requesting from them.
3. You are simply asking them to reinforce what you know. Likewise, they are apt to believe that you should know, and if you don't you are not being honest with them.

It is always assumed by the staff that an adminiatrator knows what is going on. It is taken for granted you have vast sources of information which are not available to them. If you're obviously not worried in a situation, why should they be? This is not disloyalty. It is normal, human behavior.

THE
NEED
FOR INFORMATION

However, this human behavior makes the job of gaining accurate managment information and problem solving more difficult. Management has a craving for accurate information.

The
Laws
and
Principles
of
People
Management

Computers, copiers, and communications equipment all exist because management wants and needs more accurate and detailed information as quickly as possible. Yet, a leader can't expect this kind of complete and accurate information from subordinates, especially if these subordinates are involved in a situation.

Equally important, an administrator can't be disappointed in a staff or offend a subordinate because of this fact. A leader simply cannot and must not let the management need for information impair the relationship with those being led. Perspective can be maintained if you remember never to expect or demand one of your colleagues to act against his own best interest. Your task remains filtering and evaluating information received to gain a total and accurate picture of any situation. The problems come when a leader ignores the teachings of the Law of Filtered Information and acts and reacts out of information received from a small or select group of subordinates. The whole truth usually does surface in most situations. However, accurate information "after the fact" does not help any leader lead.

Every good leader needs information. We all recognize that, to a large degree, the effectiveness and acceptance of accurate information facilitate good administrative decisions. Modern technology has provided us with electronic equipment that gives us every conceivable kind of information we need quickly and accurately. It has greatly aided the decision-making process. But computers are most often used in relation to the technical side of management. Usually, we rely on our staff to give us valuable and necessary information on the human side of management.

To gain information, most administrators have found an "open-ended" and "open-door" policy has provided a valuable source of information. More often than not, though, we have a few "select" people whom we rely on to give us accurate, truthful, and objective information. As every leader knows, this can be a help or a hindrance. Most have experienced greater difficulty in problem solving situations because the information received from a subordinate was partial rather than total. That's why every leader needs to be aware of the Law of Filtered Information. Remember, this is not a principle of management with exceptions to the rule. It is a law.

THE
THEORY
OF RIGHT/WRONG CONFLICT

*Rationale: The attitudes, opinions, and beliefs of those being
led cannot be overlooked regardless of the opinion
management holds regarding staff attitudes,
opinions, and beliefs.*

Administrators are concerned with making sound decisions.
We do not want to make mistakes. We are very concerned
about such things as right and wrong, good and bad, correct
and incorrect. Unfortunately, our concern often leads us to do
and say the wrong things in the leadership role.

Right and wrong, good and bad, correct and incorrect have
meaning to management only insofar as they indicate to management what adjustments administrators must make to
change the attitude and behavior of those being led. A leader
must never forget that how people "think" is the real issue in
any situation. It outweighs all other considerations. That is, it
does if administrative leadership beliefs and proposed changes
are to be accepted and effective. Once management knows
how people "think," a plan or course of action to enable acceptance can be initiated. Without such consideration, we are
likely to "plow ahead" without the support of those we lead.
When we do, failure rather than success becomes the probability.

Too often, management judgments regarding the attitudes,
opinions, and beliefs of a staff keep us from approaching
problems, much less solving them. When management does
judge someone's thinking as "wrong," somehow a leader can
and will walk away from that person and problem with the
rationalization that "I'm right — he's wrong." Then, they can
begin believing that management "can't" or "shouldn't" do
anything about it. This is a management error. What we have
forgotten is that right or wrong is insignificant in comparison to
relating to people and solving the problem at hand. It is simply
not the issue for management.

If your people "think" you're unfair as an administrator —
you might as well be. Whether you are or not is insignificant.
And you had better meet this problem or it will grow. It does
absolutely no good for a principal, for instance, to prove to the
superintendent or explain to his staff why he is not unfair. The

The
Laws
and
Principles
of
People
Management
only good that can happen is for management to treat the issue.

Failure to accept the theory of right/wrong conflict reflects a failure to accept many other management laws, such as the Law of Positive Reinforcement and the Law of Total Responsibility. Failure to recognize the importance of this theory is often the beginning of the end to an administrative career. It need not be. It won't be, if leaders will remember to react professionally rather than personally to issues and criticisms and respond in a positive way to how people "think" rather than what management regards as right or wrong.

THE
THEORY
OF GROUP COMMUNICATION

*Rationale: Management communication must be arranged
and presented in such a manner that messages
offered contain personal impact upon the life
style of the listener, or only partial listening will
result.*

I have stated repeatedly that achieving understanding is a
constant leadership problem. Everyone says the other person
doesn't understand. In many ways this is true. People often do
not understand the communications they hear. Yet, all management laws relate emphatically that the responsibility for
achieving understanding lies at the top. It rests with the administration. However, there are two primary reasons why a professional staff does not understand administrative communications.

    A.   They aren't interested.
    B.   They don't listen.

PERSONAL
IMPACT
PLUS ... RESPECT

Most certainly, it is recognized that an administrator can't
force people to listen or be interested. Too, we all know that no
administrator can influence everyone, every place, all the time.
Yet, we also know that every administrator can change both the
communication approach and technique to gain a better success average for listening, interest, and understanding. What
every leader must know and appreciate is that if he wants
someone to understand something, he must work hard to explain it — and take definite steps to make sure he is reaching
people with his message. This is not as difficult as one might
think, because some important facts are known about communication.

Communication will be discussed again later in this book.
However, in relation to the Theory of Group Communication,

The
Laws
and
Principles
of
People
Management

there are two very important facts that a leader must be aware of when planning to talk to groups. These facts are the primary reasons why professional teachers don't listen to a speaker in group situations. A leader cannot ignore or discount the reality of their existence.

1. People truly don't believe what is being discussed pertains to or affects them personally.

2. People believe their own opinion, belief, or judgment is superior to that which is being offered by the speaker.

That's why the following administrative techniques facilitate group listening.

1. An administrator must arrange the message so that it has a personal impact on the life style of the listener whenever and wherever possible.
2. An administrator must have the respect of the staff, or listening is impaired. Respect is best facilitated by planning, preparing, knowing what you're talking about — and knowing whom you are talking to.

TWO
VITAL
FACTS

The Theory of Group Communication teaches us two basic concepts. First, you are always speaking to individuals even when talking in group situations. Secondly, when administrative communication has personal impact and subject matter competency, leaders can — in many ways — either command listening or deprive those we lead of a secondary need if they don't. That's a hard statement, but a truthful one. Leaders do it consciously or subconsciously daily when those they lead do not listen to their urgings or follow their directions. The problem for a leader does not come if he is severe when he should be. The problem arises if he is not severe when he should be. Most certainly, a leader can't deprive those being led a primary need like food or shelter because of their reluctance to listen and act on our orders. But we can withhold a secondary need such as love and praise. This, of course, is dependent upon how much your staff cares whether or not that you love, praise, or honor them.

THE
LAW
OF REAL TRUTH AND TIME

Rationale: In problem situations, during the process of discovering and sorting out the real truth regarding staff attitudes, opinions, and beliefs, the passage of time can magnify the problem.

As a leader, it is so easy to be misled. If a leader could discover and determine the real truth quickly in problem situations, the solving of problems would be much easier. Management is dependent upon input. Science has helped us in one area of management but hasn't done much for us in the other areas. Through computers we receive reliable technical information — in quantity and very quickly — which enables us to make good decisions quickly and efficiently.

THE
TIME
LAG

However, modern equipment cannot help us as readily with input on the human side of management. This fact presents an administrator with a very real and formidable obstacle. Good management teaches that:

1. Management must know the attitudes of the people they lead.
2. Management must determine real truth in all situations.
3. Management must resolve problems efficiently and quickly.

Yet, human behavior makes this difficult for administrators to do. Every leader must be aware that there is a "time lag" between when a leader becomes aware of the problem and when the problem is dealt with. This "time lag" may result in larger problems — if the attitudes, beliefs, and opinions of the staff are not dealt with swiftly.

Every leader must be cognizant of the fact that people form opinions during a "time lag." Worse, during these time delays,

The
Laws
and
Principles
of
People
Management

they get personally committed by word and deed to courses of belief and action. Because there is often no administrative communication or action with those being led until all the facts are known, this reality is intensified. Unfortunately, once an individual or even an entire staff gets committed to certain beliefs about a situation, changing their attitude may be difficult. In truth, teacher-attitudes formed during the "time lag" are arrived at without total information and may be formed about situations they don't fully understand. Often, teachers can't find a way out of the attitudes, beliefs, and opinions they expressed to others during this time. Then, they hold to their judgments later, even if they don't agree with them at a later time. In addition, many varied individual commitments about one issue can develop during the time lag, and a leader may be forced to deal with several problems rather than just one.

TAKE IMMEDIATE ACTION

The Theory of Real Truth and Time relates that problems should be dealt with when they are identified, or time can — and in all probability will — complicate and magnify them. Problems do not go away — even if they are unmentioned, or people seem to have forgotten them — unless they are resolved. Rather, problems have a way of intensifying. Also, the cumulative effect of such situations — even if the problems are small — can result in a complete breakdown in the acceptance of leadership. That's why an administrator can never delay gathering truth about a problem immediately. When we do, we are likely to end up dealing with several problems rather than one.

APPLY THESE PRINCIPLES

I must emphasize at this point that the three preceding chapters on the Laws and Principles of Management will be of no value to any of us, as administrators, unless we are willing to actively incorporate and practice them in our leadership plan.

These principles need to be taken off the drawing-board and applied day-in and day-out consistently, before positive and dramatic effects will take place in the institution where we have the delegated responsibility for success.

Once we have committed ourselves to the fact that leadership means "total responsibility," and once we have seen our position relative to this commitment honestly and sincerely, we will be causing ourselves to become real leaders, in the full sense of Human Management, and make it possible for our staff to appreciate and cooperate in the fulfillment of these goals. Nothing could ever be more satisfying for an administrator than to see his or her own leadership plan, centered in these Laws and Principles, come to full fruition.

CHAPTER

8

A
LOOK
AT
PROBLEMS . . .
AND
SOLUTIONS

It's an absolute fact that the vast majority of problems that confront a school administrator involve people. Knowing how to handle people problems in the best interests of all concerned is what Human Management is all about and is why we have devoted study to the Law and Principles. Those administrators who practice Human Management have realized, fundamentally, that solving problems is one of the primary functions they have been hired to serve. This realistic assessment is one we should all have. It's certainly understandable that nobody wants problems. Yet problems are inevitable. Avoiding problems or pretending that they'll go away is simply unrealistic. Problems need to be resolved; and if we don't insure their resolution, I guarantee you that no one else will.

A LEADERSHIP PROJECTION

How many times have you heard a teacher or another administrator say, "I don't want any problems." How often have you thought, "Don't bring your problems to me" or "I can't handle everything; why tell me?" The net importance in our attitude toward problems is that it affects both us as leaders and others who are in our leadership orbit. If we project a negative attitude toward problems and those who have them, we cannot be anything but ineffective leaders at best. We may find that people hide feelings and truth from us. Because of our negative attitude toward problems and those who have them, staff members may not relate complaints heard, and students may not share things with us we really need to know. Problems are the life-blood of administrators. They are one reason the administrator will always be the climate leader, problem solver, and chief executive officer of a school or school system. If we ignore or reject the reality of problems, then our staff may come to ignore or reject us as leaders.

In addition to fully recognizing and accepting the role of problem-solver, an administrator who practices Human Management understands two other significant aspects of people problems. First, he recognizes that problems do not exist until they are first identified, defined, and described by someone. Until problems surface to this point, they are nonexistent to people. An administrator who really understands this is able to eliminate a potential dilemma before it ever becomes a problem.

Many times we see a situation developing before others do. Experience alone tells us all the signs are present for the development of a situation which will, indeed, be identified, defined, and described by others as a problem in a short period of time. Students are restless, we are criticizing our teachers too much, too many of our staff are unhappy with a school rule or policy, teachers are out of the classroom or building too much, the staff is quarreling frequently, we are wasting too much time or not seeing all our staff frequently enough. Rather than face the danger signs, correct the situation, or mend a fence — we do nothing. That's a management mistake we probably would not let slip by, if we were actively practicing Human Management.

At this point, immediate administrative communication and action are musts, if we are to manage situations which will become problems. I'm not talking about partial communication with those closest to you. I'm talking about total communication on a continuous basis with every member of your school team. I call this form of communication "total penetration." Remember, problems are most likely to result from those you touch least — not those you touch most. I did not say communication will eliminate all problems. However, I did say that total penetration will reduce their number and the intensity of those which do surface. And I will say that when communication stops problems will increase and intensify. Communication and action are an administrator's greatest assets in cutting down on the number of identified, defined, and described situations — real and unreal — which become eventual problems we must deal with. Sometimes that communication and action must be extensive, and often it can be quite simple. Frequently, only a simple "I'm sorry" is needed.

The second significant aspect of solving people problems involves the acquired ability to discover the "real truth" about a given situation. When a leader can develop a professional attitude which allows seeking out and accepting the real truth, problem solving is made easier. Real truth is not only what we think — it's what others think as well. Until we can discover truth from other points of view as well as our own, problems don't get resolved.

For instance, a teacher may **not** be upset that you denied a request. The real truth may be that he thinks you dislike him. A teacher may **not** be angry because you disagreed, but because he really thinks you "put him down" in the process. Never forget, truth is the important issue, and it has two sides — yours and others.

An administrator must perceive the real truth and take communicative action quickly because, after problems are identified, people may become committed to a way of thinking. They may become entrenched by a position and consequently do and say things they would not, if they knew all the facts. This is the point where rumors flourish, misunderstandings develop, and where mountains are made out of molehills. Yet, the fact remains that if people can't find a graceful way out of their position, they may never back off. Examples in a school are countless. We have witnessed them often. The result is that we end up with several problems rather than one.

PROBLEM SOLVING
THROUGH
SITUATION MANAGEMENT

I think you can see that the very nature of problem situations dictates that we take action. But knowing "how" to take action is just as important as knowing we should! There is no more workable technique for problem-solving than Situation Management. Situation Management is the "modus operandi," the "vehicle," the "procedure" through which our understanding of the motivations of people and the Laws and Principles of Human Management can be molded into a viable leadership plan. Situation Management has a proven track record of success.

Situation Management is a step-by-step process used to solve management problems. Using the Laws and Principles of Management and your understanding of human motivation as the foundation for your beliefs, you simply use a three-step process of problem solving to assure that objective thought replaces subjective, emotional, or incomplete thinking.

One primary objective of Situation Management is to prevent management overreaction and misdirection. Also, Situation Management forces a leader to deal with only the specific problem situation and include only the parties involved in that specific problem in the problem-solving process. This process is probably corporate management's most widely used problem-solving technique. It hones in on the problem. It seldom allows magnification, and the process discourages misdirection. It is conclusive.

CASE
STUDY

Situation Management can be applied to any situation. Pick any problem you wish: a board member is openly criticizing teachers, a few teachers are absent frequently, student failures are high, teachers are unhappy about a policy, or teachers are unhappy with other teachers. Here is a simple, real, school incident. It is typical of the kind we have all experienced

134

somewhere along the line in our careers, and a good example of where Situation Management can be utilized.

Situation: You are happy. Everything is going well. You see the superintendent or a board member, and he says, "What's the matter? All I have been hearing lately is that the kids in your school are out of control." End of incident.

Your whole psyche is upset. You are angry. You are worried. You are concerned. What do you do?

1. Rush back, call a staff meeting, and discuss the situation?
2. Call certain teachers to your office and question, accuse, or reprimand them?
3. Come to an immediate decision as to who, what, and why someone talked to the superintendent?
4. See counselors and assistant principals?
5. Call an assembly and talk to students?
6. Call in student leaders and discuss the situation with them?
7. Send a letter to parents about student behavior and write a note to the staff for inclusion in the teachers' bulletin?

Don't laugh; situations like this have caused administrators to take these kinds of actions. Later, we might say, "Impossible" or "Unbelievable." Yet, hindsight often gives us different conclusions than does foresight.

The question is: What should you do?

First, retire to a quiet spot and ask yourself some questions — and answer them truthfully.

Q. Why am I concerned?
A. Superintendent or a board member is upset.

Q. Why is he upset?
A. Because kids are out of control.

Q. Is that what he said.
A. No. He said, "All I have been hearing is that the kids are out of control."

Q. Do I think that is true?
A. No.

Q. Where did he hear it?
A. He didn't say.

Here is the point where our use of Situation Management can give us the objective answers rather than subjective theories we need to solve problems. It is situations like these that can allow our imagination to run wild — and cause us grief and turmoil in the process. However, when we use objective questions like those above along with others such as: Who does he talk to? When might he have heard such talk? How do I dispel such misinformation? — we move toward solutions rather than upset and anxiety.

The value of Siutation Management has two distinct side effects. First, it helps us pinpoint the problem objectively with a minimum of time and effort. Conversations like the above are usually the result of a conversation with one person. A quick look shows us, "Oh yes, the boss saw Mr. Jones yesterday — and I know exactly what was said." Then, we can proceed to patch fences. Most importantly however, Situation Management keeps us from overreacting to these kinds of situations and involving others in them. It keeps us from causing problems where none really exist, just as often as it aids us in solving big problems. That's the real value of Situation Management, and the reason it holds a valuable place in our method of operation.

PROBLEM ANALYSIS GUIDE

The Problem Analysis Guide for Situation Management is composed of three parts: Awareness, Assessment, and Action. Remember, problem situations are occurrences which cause us to be faced with action decisions to return our life to the status prior to the occurrence. They are opportunities for both success and failure.

Awareness
1. What seems to be the situation?
2. How did I find out the situation existed?
3. What is the potential effect of this situation?
4. How serious is it?
5. How much time do I have to extricate myself?
6. Who is involved at this point?

Assessment
1. What evidence leads me to believe that the situation exists?
2. What is the specific source of this evidence?
3. Do I know that the evidence is factual?
4. Could I list steps that created the situation?
5. Whose mind must I change to resolve the problem?
6. What does that mind think now?
7. How will I know when the situation is resolved?

Action
1. Join the key individuals in the situation with the key issues.
2. State specifically: Who believes what?
3. Why do they believe this?
4. How do I change their beliefs?
5. What is the best method to use to gain this change?
6. How do I implement this method?
7. Once it is over, what steps do I take to assure that it will never happen again?

You may, of course, add to these questions. However, I think you will find that it usually isn't necessary. The Laws and Principles are our administrative guides. The steps of Awareness, Assessment, and Action contained in the process of Situation Management are excellent courses of action procedure. Through Situation Management we not only apply our practical understanding of human motivation and the Laws and Principles of Management, we also avail ourselves of a workable technique through which we may implement our leadership plan.

PART THREE
YOU AND A LEADERSHIP PLAN

CHAPTER

9

CAUSING
LEADERSHIP

In this section, we will take the discussion in the first two sections of the book and apply them practically to suggest workable methods and techniques for a viable leadership plan. In order to do this, three major ideas will be developed:

1. Why a leadership plan is so vitally important for your administrative and personal success.
2. Why an effective leadership plan must be based on the concepts of human motivation and the Laws and Principles of Human Management.
3. What are the necessary ingredients of the leadership plan you develop.

Like school administrators, corporation management executives hire new college graduates each year. They go to great lengths to hire the most capable people they can — to say the least. Yet, these corporate personnel officers don't even consider putting these new employees on the job immediately after hiring. They know extensive training will be required before these new people will be ready to take their place within the corporate structure. They know these graduates have the basic educational background to be successful. They know they are educationally prepared to learn their business — but they also realize these new people don't know and understand enough about their business yet to be effective employees. They know they have the potential to become valuable employees. But corporate management also recognizes that these new graduates can't hold their own with their secretaries — much less colleagues and customers — until they are thoroughly trained to think professionally rather than personally and are assisted by management to develop positive attitudes toward their work, their colleagues, their customers, their company, and themselves. Equally important, their professional training will be extensive at first, but it must continue for a lifetime. It has to, for it is recognized by corporate management that an individual's success is totally dependent upon continuous professional growth. Corporate management accepts the responsibility for the entire function of this training. Yet, this is often not the case in education.

A PROFESSIONAL LOSS ... TRIAL AND ERROR LEARNING

In education, which is twice as difficult and demanding as any business with which I have ever been associated, we take people out of college, hand them a textbook, and then throw them into a classroom with one-hundred and twenty different kinds of students and expect them to be master teachers. If they are lucky, they are given a day or week of orientation and training. In effect, we tell these new people entering our schools and profession to learn to become professional teachers by trial and error. That's a very difficult way to learn. It's not difficult to see why many potentially good people fail in education — miserably. It's also easy to understand why the years can "take their toll" so quickly and people choose to leave the profession of teaching so quickly. It's also easy to see why being a school administrator is more difficult than being a corporate executive.

FROM
THE
FIRST TO LAST DAY

We don't do much for the experienced teacher either. In a changing society and profession as dynamic as education, we continue to expect the experienced teacher to change and learn as he goes — on his own — or fail and accept total responsibility for his own failure. My management background makes me believe staff development is a process — not an event. That's why the process of staff development must begin on the first day of a career and can't end until retirement. It also makes me accept the belief that staff development is the function of management. In a school or school system, that means staff development is the responsibility of the administration. My question is: If administrators aren't responsible for staff development in our schools, who is?

From my first days in education, I was very much aware that both teachers and administrators were well-schooled and prepared on the technical sides of their jobs. Academically, they were well-prepared to teach or administrate. The voids for both teacher and administrator were on the human side of being a professional educator. Here, neither had received much preparation at all. Those who had reached a level of excellence did so on their own.

A
UNIQUE
PROBLEM

To compound this problem, the nature of the work of teachers and administrators hinders staff development efforts. The physical setup and the time schedule in a school almost prevent administrative assistance on a personal and continuing basis. An administrator can't talk to a teacher any time he wishes. Teachers are in classrooms with students. Neither can a teacher leave the classroom after a bad experience to relax or have a cup of coffee before facing the next task as those in business do. They are confined to the classroom all day long. Teachers can't even conveniently and consistently observe the methods and techniques of a colleague. In many ways, they operate alone. It's a fact: many teachers have never even seen another teacher teach for any length of time — if any — since their student-teaching experience. That's a handicap. Can you imagine a businessman being successful with such imposed isolation? Do you know any other professional who is forced to operate under similar circumstances? I don't.

Yet, this is a handicap inherent in teaching and the nature of schools for which administrators must make compensations. For if they don't — who will? Again, my management background makes me ask: If administrators are not responsible for teacher training and growth in a school — who is?

A PREREQUISITE FOR LEADING

That's why a school administrator must establish a program of staff development. It is a prerequisite for leading. The staff development program established by management must be an integral part of the total leadership plan. Without such a plan, an administrator is likely to be looked upon by the staff as an obstacle. You don't have to be in a school long to realize the truth in this statement. Teachers are likely to begin thinking their administrator serves no useful function. In fact, they are likely to begin to believe that they are more competent, intelligent, and significant than their administrator. When this happens, administration is no longer a function. It is merely a position. Worse, leadership is rendered ineffective. When this happens, if it weren't for the existence of school needs on the technical side of management, there would be no need for an administrative position.

I taught in an excellent school and had excellent administrators during my teaching days. But during the first years in education, I saw many things happening in our school. Maybe you did too. They were happening on a nationwide basis.

1. I saw schools becoming more teacher-centered and administration-centered than student-centered. That I rec-

ognized as violation of a Law of Management. As you know, it's called the Law of Origin. This law relates that institutions must operate in agreement with the reason for their origin and existence, or failure, rather than success, becomes the probability. Schools are for children. They are not maintained to meet the personal and professional needs of teachers. Yet, I saw decisions made out of teacher interest rather than student interest.

2. I saw many master teachers doing a great job. But I also saw the leadership on school faculties emerging from the negative members of the staff — and this negative voice was telling teachers what they should not do — rather than what they should be doing for children. Accomplishing all the work of the school was being neglected by these teachers. I did not see much opposition to this thinking. Neither did I see management doing anything to reinforce the mission of the school. This, of course, violates the Law of Positive Reinforcement. It states that in the absence of positive reinforcement from appointed leaders, negative attitudes are likely to emerge from the group being led.

3. I also saw a gap developing between teachers and administrators that was unhealthy — to say the least. Maybe one reason for this reality was the fact that teachers did not see their administrators as a source of security or as an aid in achieving personal success in their chosen profession. I didn't see any concerted efforts by management to bridge the gap either.

4. I saw administrators offering hundreds of rationalizations for not helping teachers do a better job in the classroom. I believe this was a response directly attributable to lack of preparation on the human side of management. In truth, administrators either didn't know what to do or didn't know that the human side of management was part of their responsibility.

The motivation and rationale for an administrator to establish a program of staff development lies in a simple truth. That truth is the fact that teacher and administrator success or failure — and happiness as human beings — is almost totally dependent upon their ability to develop productive relationships with the people with whom they are working. So is the

145

success or failure of the institution dependent upon human relationships.

Books, desks, and buildings don't make good schools. People do. To have effective schools, people must get along with other people. In the case of a teacher, it means the ability to develop rapport with students, administrators, counselors, parents, and the rest of the school team. As teachers, if they can't relate to these people, if they can't understand them, if they can't cause children to behave in a manner necessary to enable group instruction, they will not find success in the education profession. And in teaching — when you don't find success — failure keeps knocking at your door. It comes in the form of anger, frustration, inadequacy, and hopelessness. It causes one to make mistakes of all kinds with all kinds of people. Unfortunately, when this happens, teachers are likely to direct their personal failure back at the kids — and administrators. Likewise, teachers are likely to become negative influences on the staff. They are apt to begin disliking kids, colleagues, teaching, schools, and administrators without realizing that their attitudes emerge from their own failures. I think every administrator knows exactly what I mean.

A
NEED
FOR SKILLS

It's easy for teachers to rationalize all of their failures away by blaming children and parents and colleagues and administrators. This happens primarily because, in truth, they want so badly to be good teachers. The problem is that they don't have the repertoire of human relations skills to deal with people and people problems. Academics they know — people they don't. But you don't teach academics to people. You teach people academics.

I am convinced that the vast majority of teachers are academically prepared to teach. Those who are not successful in teaching have people problems. This is not a problem known only to education. It has been said that ninety-five percent of the people who lose their jobs in this country don't lose them because they can't do the work. They lose them because they can't get along with the people with whom they are required to

146

work. That's why a staff development program that emphasizes the human side of teaching is a management absolute.

I believe there is a giant need to help teachers with their own attitudes toward their work as classroom teachers and the work of the school. There is a need to help teachers understand the attitudes and behavior of others. There is an ever-present need to help teachers add to their human relations skills to facilitate their working with students, parents, teachers, cooks, custodians, nurses, counselors — and even administrators.

Almost all businesses have daily or weekly meetings to help their people develop and maintain a positive, professional approach to their work — and give them the tools they need to find success. Why? Because professional staff training and development is not a once-a-month or once-a-year event — it is a continuous process that should begin on the first day of a career and not end until retirement. A leader can never forget that growing professionally is a process — not an event. That's why once-or-twice-a-year inservice days will not meet this need.

In teaching, when the professional growing stops, the dying process begins. Teaching is the most dynamic and demanding of all professions. A school administrator must never forget this reality. Such a remembrance might help an administrator never fail to fulfill the continuous management responsibility of giving teachers the human tools they need to find success and satisfaction in teaching.

I would venture to say that the master teacher of ten years ago would not make it today unless personal and professional growth has been maintained. Unfortunately, too many teachers start the process of professional death after they have been in education only three to five years. I believe management must accept the responsibility for this reality. It might not happen if teachers had a leader who was a partner in the teaching process. My management background makes me believe that this is a management responsibility. This is the function of administration.

THREE
KINDS
OF LEADERS

There are only three kinds of leaders who head institutions:

1. The Creators.
2. The Maintainers.
3. The Destroyers.

Only the creators operate from a platform of total responsibility acceptance. In many ways, both the maintainers and destroyers are alike. Both lead from a negative base. The maintainers, however, erroneously think that the status quo will hold an institution on course and generate good administrator-teacher relationships in the process. Make no mistake, it will not. In truth, institutional tone, achievement, competency, and efficiency must increase continuously just to keep pace with the natural evolution of progress. The status quo in any organization — be it a family, church, business, or school — almost guarantees regression. All it needs is the passage of time.

Only the creators are the leaders who accept the reality that the moral, ethical, and professional tone of an institution is established to a large measure by the chief executive officer. Time and time again, it is proven that those being led will achieve at the pace and example of the leader. In many ways, those being led cannot be any better than their leader. Neither can the institution.

The creators who lead our schools are those who set the tone, climate, and pace for the attainment of excellence. They are also the ones who instill and generate the professional attitudes which promote a positive approach to teaching and accomplishing all the work of the school. First and foremost, those who are creators accept their position as the leaders of the institution. They understand that administration is a total function. They make decisions out of strength rather than weakness. They never lose sight of the fact that the fundamental value in a school is the well-being of students. Every leadership action and decision must support this fundamental value.

The maintainers and destroyers do not adhere to this value consistently. Their course is never clear. That's why they are just as likely to act out of weakness as their strengths.

For example, a maintainer or destroyer would not ask of a new idea, "Is it good for students?" Rather, he would more likely be concerned with whether or not staff members would accept or reject the offering. His question before acting might be, "Will teachers like it or not?" "Will it cause teachers more work?" "Is it good for the administration?" or "Will it be easy or difficult to do?" Almost everything both the maintainer and destroyer do violates the Law of Origin as well as most of the other Laws and Principles of Management.

The leadership decisions and actions of the maintainer and destroyer most often focus on the reaction of the negative factors of the school staff rather than on those teachers who are positive and progressive. They usually end up with no followers at all. The good teacher, the one whom they should be focusing on, is the one who dislikes them the most. They never have his respect. Unfortunately, they don't know why. Yet, the answer is obvious.

The big difference between the maintainer and destroyer is that the destroyer is always looking for programs and activities to eliminate. He is always looking for less to do. He doesn't want to do what is already being done. The maintainer is not an eliminator. However, neither is he adding to the services offered by the school. The status quo is his goal.

LONG-STANDING TEACHER COMPLAINTS

Effecting positive and progressive leadership is not an easy accomplishment. One thing is certain, it cannot be achieved without an administrative plan and persuasive communication. Both the plan and the communication must include offering the professional attitudes, outlooks, and perspectives needed to find success in teaching.

I believe that the key to effective leadership lies in providing help and assistance to those being led. I believe that the leadership plan must include help on both the technical and the human side of teaching. Giving administrative help on the human side of teaching is an absolute necessity — and it must include giving teachers practical and workable techniques which will help them do a better job in the classroom. That's the function of leadership and being a school administrator.

The success and happiness of an administrator is dependent upon one's ability to get all the work of the school accomplished and generate good human and professional relationships in the process. Without total communication — designed to be helpful and of assistance — with every teacher on a continuous basis, this is impossible.

Teachers have complained about administrators since the beginning of schools. Much of it is normal. Yet, teachers have five general complaints about school administrators that keep surfacing year after year:

1. Teachers complain that they cannot see, visit, or communicate with their administrator as often as they wish.
2. Teachers complain that they don't know exactly what administrators expect of them as a classroom teacher.
3. Teachers also say that they don't know what they can expect of their administrator.
4. Teachers say they don't understand how their administrator thinks — because administrators think in terms of total staff and school needs while teachers' thoughts are individual.
5. Teachers complain that they don't think their administrator is giving them any help in their work as a classroom teacher.

In many ways, these are valid complaints. A close look may reveal that many administrators do not have any kind of a leadership plan for helping their teachers in their work as classroom teachers. Many don't have any kind of continuous plan to generate good leader-teacher relationships. Many don't have any kind of plan for communicating either professional attitudes or the human relation skills needed for success in teaching. In truth, all that many administrators have done to meet these teacher objections regarding administrators is explain to a staff that the responsibilities, duties, and complexities of administration and being a school administrator seem to be forcing them to spend more time on paper work and the technical side of management.

We, as well as our staff, may be well aware that our work as an administrator allows less time than administrators need and desire to spend with teachers and students. That does not help our position as administrators. We may have good intentions to "try harder" in the future to devote more time to our teachers. Yet, we all realize that the nature of the work of the school for teachers and administrators alike works against our making this promise a reality.

The plain truth is that administrators are busy. So are teachers. Days are already filled to capacity for administrators, and with the number of people being led — from students to custodians to professional staff — personal staff help on a one-to-one basis is indeed a very difficult accomplishment. However, this fact does not absolve an administrator of leadership responsibility on the human side of management. These facts do not alter our administrative responsibility to help those we lead. Neither does it permit us to offer excuses or expect others to accept and be tolerant of our excuses. It merely indicates that we must make adjustments and compensations for this natural and normal reality which is inherent in schools.

The leader who does not make an adjustment to compensate for this handicap is like a teacher who says he can't teach because he has a discipline problem. Who is responsible for discipline in the classroom? The teacher is — just as an administrator is responsible for staff development and the creation of good administrator-teacher relationships.

THE
CLIMATE
LEADER

To be an effective leader, those being led must look to the administrator as the climate leader. They must look to this administrator for help, guidance, and direction in being a better teacher. Because of the administrative void in meeting the needs of those they lead, teachers are not looking to their school leaders. In fact, it may be the last place that many would look. The truth of the matter is that many teachers are forced to learn the skills of their profession either outside the school or system or in a program of self-development. That's the problem.

To the vast majority of these teachers, administration is looked upon more as a position than a function. Worse, they believe that the administrative position serves them in no way. That's why many look upon administrators as an obstacle rather than a bridge or educational partner. That's why the principles, tools, and motivational rationale that is the basis of persuasive communication are vital to every leader. They determine the effectiveness of communication.

**THE
TOOLS
OF COMMUNICATION**

A leader may utilize a wide assortment of tools to achieve total staff communication. Staff meetings, department meetings, weekly bulletins, newsletters, intercom announcements, and individual teacher conferences are the most common vehicles used. Too, a leader may use teaching handbooks, rules, regulations, policy statements, and other methods to provide administrative direction and communicate with a faculty. Likewise, classroom visitations, faculty socials, inservice days, notes, memos, letters, and birthday cards are just a few of the many tools of communication that one can use to effect leadership acceptance. Yet, to be effective from both an administrative and a staff point of view, all leadership communication must utilize both the principles of communication and the motivational rationale that is the basis of persuasive communication.

**THE
PRINCIPLES
AND RATIONALE**

The principles of communication are vitally important to a leader. They can never be overlooked. They should be studied thoroughly. They make valuable topics for administrator inservice workshops, seminars, and informal gatherings with a school or school system.

The primary principle of communication relates that "individual thought governs human acceptance and decision-making action." This principle is easily forgotten when attempting to lead groups of people. Once removed from the one-to-one communication situation, an administrator is apt to think this principle does not apply. It does. That's why administrative approach, method, and technique cannot change in group communicative situations.

I firmly believe that all administrative communication efforts — with individuals and groups — should be designed to influence teacher thought on an individual basis. To achieve this level of communication, only one communicative appeal must be considered: a leader must appeal to that which is important to the individual by answering "the Primary Question." Remember, everyone asks continually of every leadership request, urging, and utterance, "What's in it for me?" That's the Primary Question.

Right or wrong, good or bad, like it or not, the Primary Question is an ever-present reflection of individual thought. It must be answered as often as possible in all leadership efforts. It can never be ignored or discounted.

The Primary Question can only be answered by considered, caring, and persuasive communication which contains the fundamental value of student well-being. Never think for a moment that administrative communication which violates the Law of Origin will be effective. It will not.

Likewise, communication efforts which are regarded as orders, directives, threats, ultimatums, or demands will not create teacher-administrator rapport or generate the cooperative tone necessary for educational excellence or the acceptance of leadership. In fact, these types of administrative communication will be resisted and even fought by a professional staff.

The basis of persuasive communication is called Teacher Viewpoint Technique. This communicative technique is the most powerful because it is directed toward teacher self-attainment and fulfillment. Most importantly, it focuses on and answers the Primary Question. Teacher Viewpoint Technique should be the motivational rationale behind every leadership urging and every decision to follow leadership. One can never, even for a moment, forget this reality. An examination of many problems will reveal their source began at this point.

Teacher Viewpoint Technique and persuasive communication must be the guideposts of administrative communication. There are several factors which we, as administrators, can never forget about our leadership responsibilities when communicating with teachers.

1. An administrator can never forget that every teacher has the right to ask, "What is my administrator doing for me — personally — to help me become a better teacher?" This prerogative is answered in all the Laws of Management. Teachers, like all others being led, have a right to look for tangible evidence of administrative concern for their problems as well as concrete help in avoiding and/or solving them. Both administrative words and ac-

153

tions must answer this ever-present teacher question which is being asked individually and collectively by those being led.

2. An administrator must recognize that, in truth, a leader does not have the right to criticize, judge, or evaluate any teacher until that leader has first fulfilled the leadership responsibility of help, guidance, and assistance through instruction. This truth is also revealed in the Laws of Management. Effective leadership can only be achieved by considerate, caring, and diligent "showing the way." Facilitating the work of the classroom teacher is the function of administration.

3. An administrator must be cognizant of the fact that leadership assistance is also the foundation of teacher accountability. It's a simple truth that the specific guidelines for the attainment of excellence and the probability of success must precede accountability. Practical and workable suggestions and concrete ideas, advice, and recommendations must be offered to help a teacher gain professional competency. Administrative criticism and evaluations without help and assistance are worse than meaningless. They are detrimental to efficiency and morale and hinder meeting the needs of students and accomplishing the work of the school. That's why the programs we have adopted in recent years for teacher evaluation are ridiculous. That is, they are unless prior to such plans of evaluation, we have established strong programs of staff development. If we have not, teacher evaluation simply drives another wedge between leader and teacher. Such plans say we are their judges but not their helpers. Can you imagine how you might feel toward a leader who judged you but gave you no help? Can you imagine, too, that if help is not evident, you might think your leader is judging you and doesn't know the first thing about teaching?

4. An administrator must accept the fact that when help is absent from administrative effort, then, as far as teachers are concerned, there is no leadership at all. When leadership help is nonexistent, self-help and trial-and -error knowledge must dominate teacher learning, and approval and appreciation of leadership efforts is a difficult if

not an impossible attainment. Worse, negative staff attitudes as well as administrator-teacher relationships and credibility gaps become the probability. In fact, teachers are likely to begin to believe that administrators are incompetent, unintelligent, and insignificant. Truly, when this happens, administration is no longer a function in the eyes of teachers. It is merely a position. Then, leadership is rendered ineffective as well as unrewarding from an administrative point of view.

THE
FIVE
C'S
OF
ADMINISTRATION

There are five fundamentals necessary in every leadership plan. I call them the Five C's of Administration. They are: Competency, Cooperation, Control, Communication, and Caring. Every administrator must be aware and knowledgeable of the importance of these five elements in the leadership effort — if personal and professional success as a leader is to be found. At first glance, one might think these five elements are personal and apply only to the administrator. They do not. The Five C's are two-sided, and they reflect the direct influence of human motivational behavior as well as the Laws and Principles of Management.

COMPETENCY

Administrative competency lies in a knowledge of and the ability to apply management skills on both the technical and human side of management. The foundation for this employment lies in the Laws and Principles of Management in relation to the wants, needs, and motivations of human beings.

The Law of Total Responsibility relates that an administrator is responsible for the competency of the school team. This responsibility includes the attitudes and philosophies as well as the skills necessary for staff members to find success in teaching and to accomplish the work of the school. The competency of the entire school team is basic to success. An administrator must never forget that the team includes everyone — from teacher to administrator. The teaching staff is an administrator's greatest leadership asset. It is an asset that needs constant leadership attention and nurturing.

Many administrators assume that their professional staff is competent. Because of degrees earned, experience, and other factors, an administrator automatically comes to the assumption that the staff is highly competent. This may be a management assumption without substance. Teachers are more likely to be competent on the academic side of teaching than they are on the human side. That's a fact.

The colleges and universities have done a good job academically preparing teachers to teach. However, prior to their actual teaching days, few teachers will face the human relations situations and problems professional educators are required to face day in and day out. Because of this truth, no administrator can ever make the assumption that because a teacher has earned a degree that he is academically qualified to teach. Neither should a leader arrive at the conclusion that the staff, individually or collectively, has the skills necessary in the area of human relations to be effective teachers because of degrees earned. Nor can a leader fail to realize that upgrading teachers in the area of human relations is a constant process. These kinds of assumptions can never be made by administrators, or competency may suffer.

The human side of teaching is the difficult aspect of teaching. It is not automatic. Teachers must have a wide assortment of skills on the human side of being an educator. A teacher that cannot relate to students cannot even attempt to teach all students. On the other hand, the teacher who can relate to cooks, custodians, secretaries, counselors, colleagues and administrators is the one who will have the highest level of productivity, efficiency, and competency. As a result of having to learn professional competence in the area of human relations mostly through experience, teachers often make countless errors which they pay for time and time again. In this process, they are likely to become resentful of those who were hired to be their professional leaders — if there is a void of help from their administrators. Ultimately, administrators, teachers, and all those they serve are affected because an administrator failed to realize that teachers need continuous help in developing and maintaining professional competence on the human side of teaching. Teachers need leadership in developing this professional competency on an individual basis.

All teachers want and need administrative help, guidance, and direction in a positive and helpful way. When this individual attention and assistance is not received, negative staff attitudes are likely to emerge. That's why an administrator must assume responsibility for the competency of the school team and have a plan to assure the development of competency.

COOPERATION

Cooperation is not a natural element found within school buildings or systems. Cooperation is a learned condition. It must be taught. Administrators are the ones with the responsibility to teach it. The best way for leaders to teach it is to be cooperative themselves as well as communicate the need and the benefits derived from cooperation. Cooperation is a two-way street. It does not move in just one direction.

Often, school administrators assume that a staff will automatically develop and maintain a cooperative spirit. Management often arrives at this false assumption because they believe that those employed by the school realize that an institution can't operate without a cooperative tone and spirit. It is assumed that every staff member automatically recognizes that cooperation is a necessary ingredient in the school setting. It is taken for granted that every member of the school fully understands that the purpose of their existence is to meet the needs of students. A leader often erroneously concludes that every school staff member — whether it be cook, secretary, teacher, custodian, or counselor — automatically and fully understands at the time they are hired that the work of the school requires a cooperative effort, and their role is a cooperative venture with other members of the school team to get the work of the school accomplished. Unfortunately, many do not.

However, as a learned behavior, cooperation must be experienced in both a giving and receiving way to become a permanent condition. People need to be administratively taught — and continually reinforced by word and deed — that what is done in a school must be done for the students who attend that school. The base of a student-centered school lies in the fundamental attitude, belief, and practice on the part of the school staff that what is best for students is best for the workers of the school rather than vice versa. Herein lies our mutuality as educators and workers in the school. This is our common ground whether we are administrators, teachers, cooks, custodians, counselors, nurses, bus drivers, or members of the board of education. When any staff member forgets that individual and collective effort must be aimed at meeting and serving the needs of students, a school is in trouble. Likewise, an administrator is in trouble when he or she fails to provide the leadership guidance and direction that is needed to develop teamwork and a cooperative spirit among the staff for students' best interests.

Administrative leaders must take the initiative to guarantee the maintenance of a student-centered approach toward getting the work of the school accomplished. Certainly, maintaining a student-centered school requires a team effort. Without a team effort and cooperative staff spirit among the varied elements of school personnel, the school team can quickly become staff-centered rather that student-centered. Then a disintegration of the situation begins from within. But this possibility can be stopped before it begins — if the administration has a continuous plan which gives leadership direction toward generating cooperation and a team effort for maintaining a student-centered school. Without a plan of common purpose, neither cooperation nor a team approach toward accomplishing the work of the school has a very high probability for becoming a reality.

CONTROL

Where the authority is, the control must be as well. That's

why every leader must have control of what has happened and what is going to happen within the institution. The statement does not, in any way, imply administration dominance. Dominance will not cause others to want what you are doing as a leader. But administrative control does mean one must have an awareness, knowledge, and skill to be the source or point of reference for staff leadership. To gain this level of leadership, administrators must act in a manner which conveys to all that they assume the responsibilities inherent in the administrative post. That sounds simple, yet too many leaders want control but abandon the responsibilities that allow it. In truth, they give their leadership position away at the first hint of trouble, difficulty, criticism, or confrontation.

"Passing the buck" can become a habit for some in leadership positions. It is the primary methods used by some to give their leadership away. However, no effective and successful leader permits responsibility or blame to be passed. More importantly, no leader expects others to do his job for him by passing responsibility to them.

The fact is: administrators are hired to serve as the chief executive officer in a school or system. Those who allow all leadership responsibilities to be passed to others through blame, pretending ignorance, or by shoving decision-making to committees and department chairmen or grade leaders as a means for avoiding responsibility and possible criticism are shirking their professional responsibility in the worst possible way. They are forcing responsibilities upon others where both responsibility, authority, and control are noninherent. They will never achieve the administrative control needed to guide an institution toward productivity or excellence.

In many cases where administrators abandon their responsibilities, leadership control often reverts to staff members who don't have the authority to make decisions — and the rest of the staff knows it. That's why such responsibility often seems to end up in the hands of the weak staff members, the ones who have an "axe to grind," or those who are negative in their approach and philosophy. In almost every case, the negative will emerge when enthusiastic and positive leadership efforts are not given by the administrator hired to accomplish this task.

An administrator must have control. Control is granted by title and position. However, it can only be effected by initiating a continuous plan which reveals that leadership is coming from where the authority is. You can't have control without responsibility.

161

COMMUNICATION

If one cannot communicate, then one cannot lead. If a professional staff is expected to understand and perpetuate the necessary professional attitudes and utilize positive teaching techniques which facilitate the probability of institutional success, administrative communication is a must. Without such communication there can be no attainment of education excellence. Nor can good staff and student relationships be instilled in the process.

An administrator can't communicate enough. A leader simply can't offer too much help. That is not to say idle talk or meaningless meetings are needed. Don't read between the lines. I'm simply saying that you can't give your teachers too much help by offering practical and workable assistance for their work with students. Yet, many school leaders say, "My teachers don't want help," or "My teachers don't need help." Can you imagine the president of General Motors making that statement? I can't. I've heard administrators say, "Teachers don't use what they are giving them now — so why do more?" That's like a teacher saying, "Students aren't studying, so I'm not going to teach." Remember, the tone for everything from evaluation to excellence is established by management help. Don't let anyone talk you out of leading.

Without doubt, lack of communication causes the vast majority of teacher-administrator misunderstandings that can lead to a breakdown in leadership acceptance. Little gripes grow into big teacher-administrator problems when empathetic communication between administrators and their teachers is lacking. An administrator must have a plan which enables communication with every teacher individually and the staff as a group on a regular and frequent basis. Equally important, the plan must include communicating the same story and same image to all, or a credibility gap will result. The big criticisms from teachers come not because administrators are doing too much for teachers. They come because they aren't doing enough.

CARING

Caring is a big part of leadership — much more, I think,

than many leaders really believe. If you don't care about kids and teachers and the job our schools are trying to accomplish, you're in the wrong profession.

Administrative caring is reflected in everything we do, from the rules we write to the orders we give, to the way we talk to teachers about their problems, frustrations, and concerns. It's also reflected in how we treat their accomplishments.

How much we really care is reflected in how we treat all the workers of the school as well as the students who attend our school. All the Laws, Principles, and Theories of Management are a waste without caring. All the knowledge of human behavior and leadership techniques lose their weight and merit without caring. Without caring, they all become manipulations. People don't like to be manipulated. Most won't be.

The leader who manipulates will not find long-term success in administration. Worse, one will not find personal happiness or satisfaction in education. The whole arena of administration is a giving relationship. Our biggest task is to help our faculties give of themselves completely. The fundamental value in everything we do is to make decisions and actions which are in the best interest of students. Caring is what allows us to reach for our goal.

CHAPTER

11

THE
LEADERSHIP
PLAN

One of the highest priorities for every administrator should be the establishment of both a short-term and long-range leadership plan for helping teachers on both the technical and human side of teaching. The plan should utilize both internal and external resources.

There is a vast array of talent within every school and school system which should be used to share ideas, attitudes, methods, and techniques on both the technical and human side of teaching. Administrators, teachers, nurses, counselors, psychologists, and others can be utilized in many ways throughout the years to present internal programs of staff development. For example, administrators can give formal presentations on long-range school plans, trends in education, successful programs operating in other schools, and community resources available to the staff, just to mention a few. Each department head can do the same regarding his or her academic field of specialty. Teachers can give demonstrations to colleagues of various teaching techniques or hold small group sessions in grade and course areas to upgrade all in a certain area of teaching and learning. Counselors can hold "briefing" sessions with concerned teachers regarding how to help certain kinds of students. Counselors and other supportive personnel can hold sessions which offer feedback regarding students' feelings and opinions. All these types of inservice areas make excellent topics for positive and helpful teacher discussions. However, the internal plan must be planned and arranged by the administration. It is not the duty or responsibility of the teaching staff.

The long-range external program of staff development can utilize the vast composite of talent available outside the system too. Some will charge fees — some will not. External resources on both the technical and human side of teaching are available from our colleges and universities, as well as consultants, speakers, and community institutions and agencies which deal with children. Many insights as well as cooperative relationships between schools and others can be developed by utilizing the knowledge of judges, probation officers, police officers, doctors, psychologists, psychiatrists, and local social workers. However, the responsibility for developing the staff development plan and arranging the program again lies with the administration.

Both this internal and external program can use a wide variety of formats to arouse interest, promote learning, encourage participation, and generate a professional faculty-administration climate. One such format is the familiarization program. Whether it is an administrator explaining discipline policy and the rationale behind it or a probation officer explaining the operation and goals of his agency, this is an effective method which can be employed in staff development. In addition, demonstrations, formal presentations, group discussions, panel discussions, lecture-forums, brainstorming sessions, panel-forums, and films can be used in both the internal and external program. In addition, workshops, inservice days, seminars, and symposiums can be used effectively and provide variety in an administration's short- and long-term program of staff development.

Too, a leader must remember that faculty attendence may or may not be required for all administrative program offerings. That's why a wide variety of programs and program times can be used. The important thing is to develop a positive plan of assistance and initiate it. The important thing is that management is providing the leadership for staff development and educational excellence. Too often, leadership effort is void, and the rationalization given is "teachers don't want it," or "teachers won't use it," or "I can't get everybody together." If this is the case and a leader wants full participation — or at least good participation — then time and facilities must be made available to have staff development sessions. All the reasons given teachers for "why we don't do something" only prove one thing. We are not providing the leadership we should. Mostly, this is because we haven't developed a plan. Secondly, it's because we are influenced more by negative staff members, who "don't want anything," than we are by the positive teachers in our schools. Third, it's because we haven't allowed our plan time to succeed. If everyone does not participate in everything we arrange — and applaud our efforts — we quit. If an administrator is looking for total agreement and guaranteed participation before initiating leadership, he will never find it. Result: he or she will never do much of anything on a regular basis.

TWO
PLANS
ARE A MUST

An administrator should include two distinctly different types of programs of staff development in the leadership plan.

1. Foundation Program or Continuous Program.
2. Special Events Program.

The foundation or continuous program must be frequent and must contain the feature of being ongoing in nature. I believe that a foundation program of staff development is a leadership and teaching absolute. It sets the tone for constant leadership help and assistance. It is the foundation program that not only reinforces special events inservice meetings such as inservice days, it also establishes the climate and tone that supports all management decisions on both the technical and human side of administration.

I believe this foundation program should meet some very definite criteria as an administrative-sponsored program of staff development. The criteria and rationale which I believe must be vital considerations as a foundation program are offered in the remaining pages of this book. If administrators have the time, money, and staff to create and administrate their own program, they should. If not, they must look to an established program like The MASTER Teacher for a foundation program of staff development which is continuous and ongoing in nature. That is not a commercial. But please do allow me to say that when I was an administrator, I did get angry because everyone could define administrative problems — but few gave any practical and concrete suggestions to administrators that could be carried out effectively and economically. As you know, I saw a tremendous need for such a program during my first days in education. That's where the idea for The MASTER Teacher program of Inservice Training and Teacher Relations began. The MASTER Teacher program was designed to meet all of these requirements. I firmly believe that such a program must be inherent in the leadership plan if one is to operate in agreement with good management practices. In this book I am presenting a problem and offering a practical, workable, and economical course of action at the same time.[1] Whether you use a program like the MASTER Teacher or develop your own, the criteria I have included should be considered. They are vital to any administrator-sponsored program of staff development.

CONTINUOUS

Administration is a daily responsibility. Day in, day out, year after year, leadership is an ever-present task. So is teaching. That's precisely why an administrator needs a continuous plan of staff development and teacher relations. The presence of leadership must exist in a school. One need ask himself but a few questions to fully realize how vitally important a foundation plan is to both teachers and administrators:

- How vital is teacher presence in a classroom?
- What attitudes would students have toward teachers if help were confined to one day or one week or even one month?
- Should a teacher be a resource to a student?
- Should the student and teacher be partners in the learning process?

---

1. A brochure showing how the MASTER Teacher meets the critieria of a staff development program is available upon request.

You can change the name in the above questions to teacher and administrator and get the answers you need to realize how important a continuous plan of staff development is to teachers as well as leaders. The administrator should be as vital in the teacher-administrator relationship as the teacher is in the teacher-student relationship. If not, something is wrong.

Too often, a leader's plan includes provisions for the physical things teachers need such as buildings, desks, equipment, and books — but excludes helping them in their relationships with other people. This is paradoxical — for people are always more vital in the scheme of education than are things.

In truth, an administrator can work diligently to get a teacher new books, desks, and any other physical object. Yet, these administrator efforts may never change a negative teacher attitude into a positive one. These efforts may never make a teacher feel any differently toward administrators. In fact, sometimes it may seem that teachers grow less appreciative, cooperative, and understanding of the work and effort of administrators with each passing day. Often, only more teacher "wants" emerge immediately. The wise leader learns quickly that people growth, not material growth, is the vital aspect in developing the administrator-teacher relationship. That's why every leader needs a continuous plan for staff development and staff relations on the human side of teaching. A staff development program must deal with teacher attitudes and must recognize that changing negative staff attitudes is not an overnight process. The professional growth of a teacher is a process, not an event.

A staff development program must be continuous. After all, the work of the school is constant. That's why inservice training for teachers is an administrative process that should begin on the first day of a teacher's career and not end until retirement. In any profession, you either get better or you regress. You grow — or the dying process begins. That's a fact. Not only does every leader need a constant program of assistance and guidance, but also teachers need continuous help and encouragement. Don't forget, teachers won't develop the positive and professional attitudes needed toward their work, their colleagues, or themselves in once-or-twice-a-year meetings. This can only be achieved through continuous administrative communication. That's why a foundation plan should offer assistance on a regular basis throughout the entire school year. Teachers can't exist with administrative help given only twice a year. They need help throughout the entire school year. The same is true regarding administrative assistance in the areas of teaching and human relations skills. Teachers need help on a regular and dependable basis. Only through a continuous program of staff development can administrators fill this staff need.

COMPREHENSIVE

Sometimes I think even we in education forget how complex education is — and how many different kinds of things we need to do well. To have thirty or more children in a room hour after hour and day after day with the responsibility of providing individualized instruction and care is not an easy accomplishment. In addition to being able to do the common things uncommonly well, a teacher must have a wide range of academic and human relations skills. A teacher faces more kinds of problems in a day than some professionals face in a month. They must be a "jack of all trades" — as well as a "master of all." That's why the foundation program of staff development must be comprehensive and deal with the wide range of needs and topics that are of concern to teachers. The special events program may deal with specifics. The foundation program must be comprehensive. A teacher's work is widely diversified. Therefore, administrative assistance must be comprehensive and deal with the wide range of topics and areas that cause teacher problems and concerns. You must offer help in the areas of discipline, staff relationships, student motivation, parent relationships, and professional attitudes as well as provide practical and workable methods and techniques.

An administrator must never forget that in many ways teachers "teach alone." They must operate as a separate entity within the whole of the school and system — in a situation where teamwork and cooperation are asked and required. All too often teachers feel they are required to learn much of their expertise by trial and error. It is a very difficult way to learn. Without feeling the presence of administrative concern and sympathy along with tangible evidence of administrative help and assistance, teachers can develop strong resentments toward administrators very quickly. Yet, with such help, they can develop strong professional attachments.

An administrator must attempt to give tangible evidence that they are trying to take some of the trial and error out of the lives of teachers. Most administrators realize that teacher problems, concerns, and frustrations cover the broad spectrum of the work and decisions of the school too. Therefore, a foundation program with a wide base meets one need while the special events program gives offerings at special times throughout the year. Both programs then reinforce each other. Not only is there a broad image and penetration of general administrative knowledge and understanding revealed by the two programs, but also the tone for acceptance of both programs is set and administration is then looked upon as a function.

INDIVIDUALIZED
AND
PRIVATE

To promote good administrator-teacher rapport and facilitate maximum teacher learning and acceptance, a staff development program cannot confront those it serves. It must be offered as an administrative aid, not as an administrative club. We are partners in the education process — not opponents. That's why a staff development program should provide administrative direction and helpful assistance — not criticism or pressure. For maximum acceptance and productivity, the foundation program should be as individualized and private as possible. Large group meetings may follow either an individualized or small group plan. However, the smaller the group, the better. If possible, groups should be avoided in favor of individualized and private inservice. In this way, the Primary Question is answered on an individual teacher basis.

This vital aspect of the foundation plan is tremendously important. The individualized and private aspect of teacher development also helps one not to resist the training. More importantly, private inservice eliminates one individual teacher's need to react negatively in defense to the inservice offering and affect others in a negative way. Instead, a teacher can just absorb the administrative instruction.

Individual members of the staff can affect each other in a negative way in large group meetings. That's why I do not recommend that administrative foundation programs always have group sessions. Private and individualized inservice practices help support administrative goals by building administrator-teacher rapport on a one-to-one basis. Remember, individual thought governs the decision-making process. One should utilize this principle of communication whenever possible. That's why group sessions can follow private instruction. Individual opinions are formed and those who are positive are better equipped to neutralize those who are always negative.

Administrative efforts of help must never — under any circumstances — appear as a "club" or "directive." even when group discussion follows private inservice, an administrator need not be drawn into conflict. Rather, here is the opportunity just to listen to teacher comments as a third person. Never forget, private help gives teachers the support as well as the tools they need to continue operating in professional excellence.

A
FOUNDATION
FOR ACCOUNTABILITY

Any administrative-sponsored program must contain the foundation for accountability and the measurement of performance. It is my firm belief that management does not have the right to evaluate, criticize, judge, or reprimand anyone unless it has first fulfilled its function of instruction. That's a Law of Leadership that cannot be violated.

When administrators evaluate teacher performance without providing tangible assistance, they are likely to be regarded as enemies by those they lead. It's not difficult to see and understand why. This is a common mistake many in leadership positions fail to realize. With the authority of administration comes the responsibility to help those being led. The responsibility to help always precedes the responsibility to evaluate. We are the partners of those we lead — not their judges.

That's precisely why a wide variety of concrete teaching and human relations methods and techniques must be offered in a foundation program of staff development. These methods and techniques must be designed to help teachers cope with their personal and professional day-to-day workings with students, colleagues, parents, and all whom they touch in their work. The foundation program must also help teachers deal with their own attitudes, behaviors, and beliefs as well as the professional attitudes and beliefs necessary to accomplish the work of the school. It is the providing of workable assistance that creates total leadership acceptance, and it is the foundation program which promotes the administrator-teacher relationship as a team endeavor and partnership in the learning process for students and the educational process of schools and schooling.

ONE
SIDE ...
ONE COMMITMENT

Without reservation, there are no sides in education. We are all on the same team whether we are administrators, teachers, counselors — or custodians. We have common goals and educational philosophies — and teachers need to be made aware of this vitally important fact. Without a foundation program of assistance, they will not be. Teachers need constant direction toward providing a student-centered education and workable assistance to make these theories work. There are few teachers who enter our profession who do not have the "heart" to be good teachers. There are few who do not want to be excellent teachers. More often than not, they don't know how to find teaching success. They keep making the same mistakes without realizing they are. Teachers don't need a noncontributing evaluation from administrators. They need help. They need someone they can turn to and rely on for help. If continuous help is given by management, then — and only then — does management have the right to evaluate. When management fulfills this responsibility, they are likely to find that their suggestions are appreciated and their leadership welcomed.

Teachers have the right to expect help in finding success from their leader. The foundation plan must add administrative weight to the recognition of the need for continuous teacher growth and improvement, if success is to be found — or maintained. The plan should reflect administrative eagerness to help teachers responsibly find and enjoy professional success.

SUPPORTS
ADMINISTRATIVE
GOALS

A staff development program should support both administrative goals and leadership action. Without reservation, administrative goals should be the creation and maintenance of student-centered schools, and the accomplishment of all the work of the school which is inherent in this commitment. Too, I trust a part of these goals is to effect positive leadership and generate good administrator-staff relationships in the process.

To achieve these primary objectives, a staff development program sponsored by the administration must have continuity and professional direction. It cannot "blow like the wind" in one direction and then another. It can't reflect one direction of priorities then switch to another. It can't reveal one educational philosophy, then another — depending upon the circumstances or needs of administration. This requires that an administrative-sponsored staff development program contain a common thread. The common thread for staff development and the rationale behind it must be the maintaining of student-centered schools and teacher attitudes, commitments, and actions which are in agreement with this belief.

Students are the reason for the existence of school and teachers. They must also be the reason for teacher commitment — and administrative leadership direction. All administrative guidance must reinforce the student-centered school philosophy. It must also reinforce every positive administrative action taken to meet the needs of students as expressed by both the management decisions and decision-making process used to achieve this end.

TOTAL
PENETRATION
SIMULTANEOUSLY

A staff development program must offer a vehicle which allows total administrative communication and penetration simultaneously to every member of the organization. Partial or selective communication is a leadership error. In truth, it is one of the primary causes of many administrative problems.

When an administrator fails to offer total communication to every teacher simultaneously, a division of staff interests, commitments, and loyalties become the probability. That's why total communication is a vital leadership advantage and is a must for any program of staff development.

The continuity and total communication feature of a staff development program is an aspect that an administrator shouldn't minimize, overlook, or ignore. No teacher should ever be left out. Administrators often get discouraged because their efforts are not appreciated or criticized. Yet, exclusion of a few teachers is often the cause of this dilemma. Partial communication often lies at the root of a wide assortment of administrative problems. A leader's responsibility is to all. That's why an administrative-sponsored program should include every member of the staff.

Communication is not the responsibility of others. It is the responsibility of management. All need to be offered leadership help and assistance on an equal basis. Administrative leadership help cannot be reserved for a selected few such as new teachers, those who request help, or those experiencing problems. This is true regardless of any situation or circumstance. That's why total penetration simultaneously to every member of the school team is a vital asset in an administrative-sponsored program of staff development.

EASILY
ADMINISTERED

A foundation plan should be easily and conveniently administered. Administrators are busy. So are teachers. The less complicated the program is — the more likely it is to be successful as well as continual. Private and individual help is not an easy accomplishment. Neither is administrative follow-up.

Time is valuable. It is scarce in a school for both teachers and administrators. The reality of any staff development foundation plan is that it can get shelved, delayed, or postponed because of a lack of available administrative and staff time. That's why ease of administration must be a primary consider-

The
Leadership
Plan

ation. Likewise, a staff development program should not detract administrators from other management endeavors. That's why ease of administration is important from both leader and teacher viewpoints.

PERSONAL
FOLLOW-UP

All staff development plans must contain a follow-up feature. Follow-up strengthens and reinforces all administrative efforts. Follow-up also adds significance and meaning to the initial general management effort. Therefore, if the foundation plan has follow-up features, it has added value.

Most importantly, the foundation plan should reflect that the assistance is "from administrators to teachers." The foundation plan should make teachers aware of the help being given. It should denote, "You are important, your work is important, and you are important to me." Follow-up is a vital consideration of the staff development plan, for it strengthens both the inservice program and the teachers' attitudes toward the administrative offering — as well as the individual administrator.

SUPPORTS
EXISTING
EXCELLENCE

Often, administrative efforts are necessarily devoted solely to teachers experiencing problems. This reality is derived out of management thinking. This is where the bulk of their time and energy must be spent. Yet, one of the biggest myths and errors a leader can make is to believe that some staff members need help and others do not. All need help. Some just need help from their administrators in a different kind of way.

Those teachers who carry on day after day demonstrating master teacher performance are often ignored — or they believe they are. This reality does not strengthen administrator-teacher relationships with those a leader needs allegiance with the most — the good teacher. This is unfortunate because the good teacher is the backbone of the teaching staff. Administrator success in accomplishing the work of the school is dependent to a great extent on the quality of the relationship between the good teacher and the administration.

A foundation program must serve as constant support and recognition for the master teachers on your staff. This positive reinforcement and administrative acknowledgement to existing excellence is vitally important to the success of any leadership plan. Without constant support, the master teachers on a staff are likely to believe their administrator neither cares nor is aware of their efforts. That's why the foundation plan of staff development should give recognition to the excellence demonstrated by the master teachers on the staff. A student-centered program always does.

**EASILY
SUPPLEMENTED ...
FOR
STAFF AND
ADMINISTRATOR ALIKE**

The foundation plan should be such that it is easily supplemented. The plan should not be so rigid or narrow that it limits administrators from making additions, adding a personal touch, or supplementing the effort with similar efforts on the special events staff development program. Rather, the foundation program should give a leader more room to operate.

The foundation plan should also be designed to facilitate supplementation by individual teachers as well as other administrators. That's why the foundation program should have a student-centered base. It should also provide for the sharing of attitudes, techniques, methods, and philosophies for the adoption by individual teachers in their classroom situation.

STAFF ACCEPTANCE

It is doubtful that any administrative sponsored program will be received, accepted, and approved by the entire staff with total acclaim. Regardless of need, some teachers will use and appreciate the assistance more than others. Never forget the myth of the perfect plan. You are the leader. You should know what needs to be done to meet your responsibility to create the climate for leadership acceptance. You must be concerned with fulfilling your responsibilities as a professional school administrator rather than doing nothing, because all won't totally appreciate something you are doing.

Certainly, every leader wants to plan a program which will be received by the majority and grow in acceptance. That's why you must make sure that the planned program is carefully presented to: suggest rather than dictate, praise rather than condemn, appeal rather than command, share rather than impose, counsel rather than tell. Too, you must make sure your plan is totally honest in terms of being in agreement with sound educational practices on the human side of teaching.

The plan should give the average teacher continuous support and encouragement to act out of their strengths rather than their weaknesses. When the climate for excellence is established, the average teacher will follow. Never forget, these are the teachers who will swing to the positive or the negative depending on the presence or absence of continuous, positive leadership. That's why without a program of staff development, a leader is at the mercy of the negative and the critics.

CONSISTENCY

An administrative sponsored program must be consistent. Sometimes, because of time and events, the best laid plans never get off the ground or are found too difficult to perpetuate. Yet, "spotty" assistance reflects upon administrators in a negative way. Announcing big plans at the beginning of the year — then halting or postponing for any reason casts shadows on the ability of a leader.

The foundation program of staff development must be consistent. It must reflect stability of management. It must give security. Remember, this is one of the primary purposes behind the establishment of the program. A special events program will not give leadership assistance the consistency that must be a part of the leadership plan.

THIRD
PERSON
SUPPORT

A third-person support is a vital leadership tool. It is probably the most significant asset overlooked by leaders. We use it frequently in our personal lives, but usually not as frequently as we could and should in our professional roles. Yet, third-person support offers an immeasureably valuable leadership reinforcement. It can always be used to support decision-making actions. Third-person supports pave the way for new ideas and the acceptance of new ways of doing things. Third-person supports let a leader say things that they often can't under certain situations. A leader needs to ask but one question to see how vitally important third-person supports can be: "Can you imagine how valuable it would be to have someone else tell your staff what you are telling them all year long?"

Business uses third-person supports often. We should too. The auto maker shows employees what the others are doing to support what they have decided to do. They relate what other businessmen say about vital issues ranging from increasing productivity to wages. They offer trends of economists, changing customer habits, and statistics which support their decisions and pave the way for a staff acceptance of their leadership teachniques. Leaders of education need the same advantage. That's why the foundation program of staff development should reinforce and strengthen the administrative position and decision-making process. The third-person support feature included in the staff development program can pave the way to easier management with fewer conflicts. Mostly, it aids acceptance of a leader's course of action rather than automatic rejection. In truth, third-person supports "prove the boss is right." They help people follow.

ECONOMICAL

I believe the program should be economical simply because that's the reality of school budgets. I believe that a school system cannot afford to spend less than one day's wage per teacher in upgrading a staff on both the human and technical side of staff development. Equally important, I believe the expenditure should contain both a base or foundation program and special events program.

Once-or-twice-a-year programs of staff development are not adequate from either leader or teacher need or viewpoint. Teachers need help continually throughout the entire year. A foundation program of staff development which features continuous help sets the tone and climate where administrators are looked upon as a resource. Using a base program with special emphasis on inservice days gives more meaning to both efforts.

12

THE
ADMINISTRATIVE
STANCE

Administration should not be a defensive position. There's nothing in the word **leader** that denotes a defensive stance. Quite the contrary. However, it is only through employment of the Laws and Principles of Management and an understanding of human behavior that a leader can effect positive and constructive leadership by motivating people to meet their professional responsibilities.

How leadership is approached is an individual matter. The choice of whether or not to establish a plan on the human side of leadership is made by individual choice too. That decision would be an easy one if an administrator asks but one question: Is it better for students, teachers, and the school itself to have an administrative-sponsored program of staff development — or is it better not to have a program and leave this responsibility to teachers?

SOCIAL
AND
PROFESSIONAL

When answering this question, never think for a minute that "social" contacts with teachers will fulfill this need or meet the responsibility for staff development which is inherent in the responsibilities of management. They will not. In fact, the administrator who is "socially enjoyable" and counts on coffees, visits, birthday cards, teas, and picnics to sustain his or her relationships with those being led wears thin very quickly. Don't allow such rationalizations as "We don't need help," or "All my teachers are qualified," or "We don't have time," or "My teachers don't want help" to allow you to decide not to establish a continuous plan of staff development either. All teachers need help. Whether you realize it or not, the good teachers need it most. How do you think they are maintaining their excellence? I'll tell you. They're fighting and searching and digging every minute on their own to acquire the methods and techniques to achieve teaching excellence. They take night courses, attend lectures, read professional literature, join professional organizations, and go back to school during summer vacations. Teaching is their life — and they work at getting better continually.

ADMINISTRATIVE
RECOGNITION
OF EXISTING EXCELLENCE

It's the good teacher who needs administrative recognition, appreciation, and support for performing day after day in the best interest of students and the school. They also need administrative help in their search for educational excellence. They need a partner in the teaching and learning process.

The good teachers are often the quiet ones. They seldom say, "Look how good I am." Too often, they are forced to sit and listen as others support poor teaching and human relation practices. They are forced to watch as negative colleagues tell others "what not to do for students" while they perform in an opposite manner. That's not an easy thing to do. But they do it. How do you think they feel about an administrator who is not the climate leader and who is not providing a positive base of student-centered leadership instruction?

PROVIDING
A
TONE FOR EXCELLENCE

Not only do teachers need leaders who help them learn, they also need leaders who create a positive and constructive tone which provides a climate conducive to educational excellence. If an administrator thinks good teachers can continually perpetuate excellence without help, he is mistaken. Continuing in excellence requires continuous growth. The good teachers in a school are getting help anywhere they can find it. You can be sure of that. They should be getting it from their administrators.

The average teacher needs help too. If they do not receive administrative help, it is more likely these teachers will act out of their obvious weaknesses rather than their potential strengths. That's our humanness revealed. When an administrator establishes the climate for excellence and shares the methods and techniques which enhance teaching success, then teachers will follow in a professional manner. However, teachers will swing to the positive or negative depending on the presence or absence of continuous, positive leadership with professional help and assistance.

We all know that the teacher who is experiencing difficulty needs our help. What we might not realize is how effective our help can be — if a positive and professional tone is the school climate. There are few teachers in this profession who do not have the "heart" to be good teachers. That's important. If someone wants to be good, he can be helped. It's those teachers who "don't care" who are the difficult ones to motivate. Fortunately, most teachers want to be good. They wouldn't stay in teaching if they didn't. There are simply too many frustrations and disappointments in teaching for the poor teachers to stay if they didn't desire to be good teachers. More often than not, they don't know "how" to find teaching success. They keep making the same old mistakes, having the same old problems — and they don't know why or what to do about it. Like all teachers, they need administrative help and guidance. Their need is just more obvious. An administrator must ask, "What continuous and comprehensive effort am I making to help all my teachers — the excellent, average, and poor?" If, by choice, an administrator doesn't think all teachers need the help of their administrators, a second question should be asked. "If teachers don't need any help, then what is the reason for my existence as the school leader?"

CREATING
EQUAL
OPPORTUNITY

The school staff is our biggest investment. People are also an administrator's primary asset. Most certainly, the teacher is the vital element in the learning process — and students are the beneficiaries of this asset. We need to protect and develop this asset and make it as productive as we possibly can to assure the best possible education for every student. This is Human Management. This is the function of school administration. If we hold that the fundamental value in every administrative action and decision is the well-being of students, then surely we realize the overwhelming need to help our teachers function as master teachers.

The management of business has a big advantage. They have given it to themselves by training their people continually from the minute of hiring until the day of termination. We need the same advantage as educational leaders. If you're one of those who say, "We're not big enough or don't have the money to do what we need to do," look again. How many businesses or institutions in your town or city employ more people, have more assets, determine larger budgets, or are bigger than you are? Not many. Only our thinking and priorities need revision. The decision is yours . . . the success of your teaching and school or system depends upon it — and so does yours.